ROMANS

A STUDY MANUAL

ROL

Presbyterian and Reformed Publishing Company
Phillipsburg, New Jersey

Manufactured in the United States of America

Library of Congress Cataloging-in-Publication Data

Rogland, Robert, 1941–
  Romans : a study manual.

  Bibliography: p.
  Includes index.
  1. Bible. N.T. Romans—Textbooks. I. Title.
BS2665.5.R64 1988   227′.1′0076   87–32892
ISBN 0–87552–403–6

CONTENTS

IV. CHRISTIAN LIVING

INTRODUCTION

Paul's letter to the Romans is the most comprehensive statement of the gospel of Jesus Christ found in the Bible. Particular doctrines may be dealt with in more detail in other books of Scripture, but in Romans we have the most complete, systematic presentation in one book of the foundational truths of God's plan of salvation and of the elements of the Christian life. Everyone who desires a mature understanding of the system of truth taught in the Scriptures should attempt to master the Book of Romans.

Romans: A Study Manual is intended for all who wish to work toward a mastery of Paul's letter. This manual is meant to provide Bible students, especially those who may have a limited background in Bible study and theology or who possess few other helps, with the resources and direction needed to undertake a profitable and rewarding study of Romans. Suitable for students of high school age and above, the manual can be used for personal study, in a Bible class, or with a study group.

CONTENTS OF THE STUDY MANUAL
This manual contains several basic helps for the Bible student:

1. Study Questions
The study questions at the beginning of each lesson are designed to help the student focus on the important elements in the passage

at hand. By searching the text (especially the verses given in parentheses) for answers to these questions, the student will be brought face to face with the truths Paul labored to make clear to his readers.

2. Study Notes

Following the study questions, the study notes for each lesson discuss difficult or disputed interpretations, questions that are likely to arise in the student's mind, important doctrines mentioned in the passage, and applications to contemporary life, work, and worship.

3. Answers to Study Questions

The answers to each lesson's study questions are found in Appendix B. They contain many additional scriptural references bearing on the subjects raised by the questions.

4. Other Helps

The manual contains various appendices at the back of the book. These include: a review of Romans providing an outline of the epistle, a list of important themes and topics in Romans, and an outline of God's plan of salvation based on Romans; a list of selected reference works for further study, and a complete index to the study notes.

HOW TO USE THE STUDY MANUAL

Romans is a book with an overall plan and logical structure. It can be best mastered when studied sequentially from beginning to end (but see *To the Bible Teacher*, below, for extended portions that could be studied independently if time precludes a study of the whole letter).

The manual was written with the assumption that its users would proceed through it lesson by lesson. The individual engaged in personal Bible study can set his or her own pace. The member of a Bible class or study group, however, should make every effort to keep up with the class schedule. If one skips a lesson or falls behind, one will miss much; for the most part, each paragraph or section of Romans builds on what has gone before.

Each lesson in the manual covers a natural or logical unit of Paul's thought. To gain a first impression of the direction and contents of the passage, you should read the specific passage from Romans prayerfully *without reference to the study questions or the notes.* Then carefully read the questions. Next, study the passage, looking for answers to the questions. Do not simply think about the answers to the questions. You will grasp the contents of the passage more thoroughly by writing down the answers in the space provided in the manual or in a separate notebook.

After completing the study questions, compare your answers with those supplied in the back of the manual. Be sure to look up all the scriptural references cited in the answers (and in the notes section). If you do not find your answers in the manual, you are not necessarily wrong. The questions and answers provided are meant to cover the most important points the passage has to make without implying that nothing else could be stated. If you are in a class and unsure whether your answers are correct or relevant, check with the teacher and discuss your answers with other class members.

Last of all, you should read the study notes on the passage at hand. Most of the notes do not discuss individual verses or answer specific questions. Instead, they deal with issues raised by the passage in whole or in part, speak to doctrinal topics, or draw implications for our faith and life. Many of the study notes go beyond the passage at hand.

The student who wants to delve more deeply into a particular passage or topic may wish to refer to a commentary, Bible diction- ary, or book dealing with a specific theological topic. The reference works listed in Appendix C are especially recommended.

TO THE BIBLE TEACHER

Romans: A Study Manual can be used with profit in an adult, college-age, or high school Bible class. Providing sudents with suffi- cient guidance for their own personal Bible study and preparation, the teacher can expect that the members will be able to discuss the text knowledgeably in class. The one prerequisite to a successful discussion class is student preparation. If most of the class members have worked through the study questions and read the answers and the notes in the book, the discussion will be enjoyable, profitable, and edifying.

A short review of the previous week's lesson by the teacher is a good way to begin each class meeting. A review refreshes the memory of the students and serves to place the day's lesson in its context within the Book of Romans. Such a review is particularly important in the study of a book that develops its arguments as logically as Romans does.

Following the review, the study questions should provide the framework for class discussion. The teacher should solicit answers to the study questions from members of the class, adding personal comments when necessary to introduce a point of importance or interest that the members have failed to mention. The leader should not feel obligated to cover all the points found in the answers in the manual, but he should make sure the major points receive attention. The teacher will also want to cite related passages of Scripture and make explanatory remarks of a grammatical, historical, or doctrinal nature. A good way to conclude the lesson is to give a short summary of the important doctrinal truths found in the passage and of their application to our own faith and life today.

If an individual or class would like to study part of Romans rather than the entire book, certain passages can be dealt with more or less independently. Chapters 1-5 deal with God's plan of salvation for the individual. Chapters 6-8 deal with the new life in Christ. Chapters 9-11 deal with God's sovereign dealings with mankind and his plan of salvation for his people as a whole. Chapter 12 deals with the individual's spiritual service to God, both in the use of spiritual gifts and in the practice of Christian virtues toward others. Chapter 13 deals with our obligations to government and toward all men.

It must be stressed that a student who does not have a firm grasp of God's plan of salvation for the individual (chapters 1-5) is in no position to appreciate Paul's teaching on the new life in Christ (chapters 6-8), on his sovereign dealings with the entire human race and his plan to save his people (chapters 9-11), or on the various aspects of Christian living (chapters 12-16).

All scriptural quotations are taken from the New International Version (NIV) unless stated otherwise.

The author expresses his sincere thanks and gratitude to Dr. Robert S. Rayburn, Richard Hannula, and Laurie O'Ban, all of Faith Presbyterian Church in Tacoma, Washington, who read and critiqued the manuscript.

May *Romans: A Study Manual* help you attain a mastery of the Book of Romans and, consequently, a deep understanding of the great doctrines of Christian faith and life that it so fully and clearly expounds.

I. GOD'S PLAN OF SALVATION FOR THE INDIVIDUAL

LESSON 1
Romans 1:1-17

STUDY QUESTIONS
1. What does Paul say about himself? (1:1)

2. What does he say about the gospel? (1:1-3)

3. What does he say about Jesus Christ? (1:3-4)

4. What is Jesus Christ's relationship to Paul? (1:4-5)

5. What is Paul's relationship to the Christians in Rome? (1:6-7, 8-10)

6. Give four reasons why Paul wants to visit Rome. (1:11-15)

7. What is Paul's attitude toward his task? Why does he have this attitude? (1:14-16)

8. What is the theme of the gospel? (1:16-17; see also 1:2-3)

9. How is the gospel message made known to us? (1:17)

10. How do we receive the righteousness of God revealed in the gospel? (1:17)

STUDY NOTES

1. Paul

The author of this book was the apostle Paul, a native of the city of Tarsus in the Roman province of Cilicia (presently southern Turkey). Paul, whose Hebrew name was Saul, was a Jew by nationality who enjoyed the legal status of Roman citizenship by birth (Acts 22:26-28). He had been brought up a strict Pharisee (Acts 26:5; Phil. 3:4-6) and had studied in Jerusalem under the famous rabbi Gamaliel (Acts 22:3). As other rabbis of his time, Paul had learned a secular trade to support himself; he was a tent maker or, possibly, a leather worker (Acts 18:1-3).

Saul the Pharisee had been a fierce enemy of the followers of Christ (Acts 26:9-11). But one day, as Saul was traveling to Damascus to initiate a persecution of Christians there, the Lord Jesus appeared to him in a vision (Acts 9:1-19). Saul was immediately converted to Christ and three days later was baptized in Damascus.

Looking back on his life without Christ, Paul concluded that everything he had once taken pride in—his Hebrew ancestry, circumcision, integrity or righteousness as measured by the law of Moses—was, spiritually speaking, garbage (Phil. 3:8-11). He no longer considered those things to be his righteousness or the basis of his acceptance by God. Instead, he trusted that God had provided a divine righteousness for him in Jesus Christ. This perfect righteousness, appropriated personally through faith in Christ, was the subject of the gospel that Paul preached for the rest of his life. It is this righteousness which Paul expounds in the Book of Romans.

When the Lord appeared to Ananias, the disciple who baptized Paul in Damascus, the Lord declared that he had chosen Paul to preach to both Jews and Gentiles (Acts 9:15). Within days of his conversion, Paul was preaching Christ with the same zeal he had formerly employed against the Lord, using his knowledge of the Old Testament to prove that Jesus was the promised Messiah (Acts 9:19-22). From that time on, Paul was engaged in controversy with his fellow Jews whenever and wherever he preached Christ.

Although we often think of Paul as the great apostle to the Gentiles (Gal. 2:2), he had been chosen to preach Christ to all men, Jews as well as Gentiles (Acts 9:15). When Paul entered a new town, he normally would preach first to his fellow Jews, turning to the Gentiles when the Jews rejected his message (e.g., see Acts 13:44-48). Paul never gave up trying to convert his own people (Acts 28:17-30). He loved them and was anguished over their rejection of Christ (Rom. 9:1-3; 10:1).

Paul knew from the time of his conversion that God had called him to preach to Gentiles as well as Jews (Acts 9:15). We do not know, however, when he first realized that his calling would lead him ultimately to Rome. He made three missionary journeys before his trip to Rome; each journey took him further westward from Palestine and closer to Rome. By the middle of his third missionary journey, if not before, Paul knew that he would eventually reach the capital of the world empire (Acts 19:21). Towards the end of this third journey, while he spent three months in the Greek city of Corinth, Paul wrote his letter to the believers in Rome. In this letter he expresses his intention to journey on to Spain after visiting Rome, taking the word of Christ to the westernmost outpost of the Roman world (Rom. 15:22-29). We do not know if Paul ever succeeded in reaching Spain. The Book of Acts ends with Paul under house arrest in Rome. According to tradition, Paul was martyred there during the reign of Nero some years later.

2. Rome in Paul's Day

The Roman Empire in Paul's day included nearly all the lands bordering the Mediterranean Sea as well as Gaul (modern France, Belgium, the Netherlands, and Germany west of the Rhine). Roman military power had made the empire secure from foreign invaders and had established peace, safety, and order—the *Pax Romana*—within its borders. Commerce between Rome and the provinces was active and unhindered. Subject peoples of many races and lanuages lived in Rome itself. Most were slaves, but many were free men. Rome was a cosmopolitan city, truly the hub of a world empire.

The Romans allowed their non-Roman subjects a good deal of autonomy in matters of local government, custom, and religion. Citizens of Rome, however, were subject to Roman law and assured of Roman justice wherever they might live. When Paul finally traveled to Rome, it was as a prisoner who had been accused by Jewish officials in Palestine and who had exercised his right as a Roman citizen to appeal directly to Caesar (Acts 25:9-12). Though some Roman officials might have been corrupt (Acts 24:24-27) and the protection of Roman law extended only to free Roman citizens, on the whole Rome took pains to ensure legal justice for all. (Rome's legal system is still the basis of jurisprudence in many Western nations today.)

In contrast to Roman law, Roman morality and religion were decaying. Educated Romans did not believe in the old gods anymore, even though many of them maintained the traditional forms and ceremonies of their fathers. Some Romans had turned from their traditional religion to religions that had entered from the East. By Paul's time, the so-called *mystery religions* of Greek origin had become established in Rome. The cult of Isis and Osiris had been introduced from Egypt, and the worship of Mithras had found its way to Rome from Persia. The Jews also were engaged in missionary work (Matt. 23:15), and a few Romans had turned to Judaism (Luke 7:5; Acts 10:1-2).

In the days of the Roman republic, more than two hundred years earlier, the Romans had been proud of their moral virtues. They had prized chastity, bravery, self-sacrifice, simplicity, and charitable treatment of the vanquished. But by Paul's day the ancient virtues had been replaced in practice by sexual vice, infidelity, personal ambition and selfishness, overindulgence, and the pursuit of luxury. Roman morals had grown corrupt, and the Romans themselves bewailed the fact. Very likely, those Romans who converted to

Judaism had been attracted by the worship of one holy God and the high moral code of the law of Moses.

Consider the parallels between the Roman Empire of Paul's day and America today: political stability and military might, internal peace and security, flourishing world trade, an emphasis on legal justice for all, a decline of traditional religion and an invasion of Eastern religions, moral corruption—and the hunger of a few for spiritual reality. We need Paul's gospel now as much as Rome did then.

3. The Church at Rome

The Book of Acts is silent regarding the origins of the church in Rome. However, Acts records other instances in which the gospel made a notable advance into a new ethnic group or geographical area through the ministry of the apostles. This fact suggests that the church in Rome may have grown out of the spontaneous activity of ordinary Christians rather than out of an organized missionary activity by the apostles or by evangelists commissioned for the task. Greeks, Jews, and others who had been converted in the East and had taken up residence in Rome, natives of Rome who had been converted while traveling or living in the eastern Mediterranean area, and the local converts of such believers would have met together for prayer, teaching, mutual comfort and exhortation, and the breaking of bread as did Christians elsewhere (Acts 2:46-47).

Whatever the origin of the church in Rome, apparently it was well established by the time Paul wrote Romans (1:8). He did not write to the Romans to convert them to Christ but, rather, to deepen their understanding of the faith. He expected that they had grown in the grace of God enough to strengthen his own faith as well (1:11-12). As we study Romans, we find that Paul takes certain basic truths of the faith—the trinitarian nature of God, historical facts of Jesus' life and death, contents of the Old Testament—as givens. He assumes the Romans know these truths and, consequently, does not expound them at length. He endeavors instead to show all aspects of the truth that "the righteous shall live by faith" (1:17).

The church in Rome contained believers from both Jewish and Gentile backgrounds. Paul explicitly declares some Christians to be Gentiles (1:13). He also refers to some as brothers who know the law, i.e., the law of Moses (7:1); most likely, he refers in that instance to fellow Jewish Christians. Priscilla and Aquila, whom he greets by name (16:3), were Jews (Acts 18:2). The presence of both Jewish and Gentile believers in the church at Rome is reflected in Paul's emphasis on the truths that both Jews and Gentiles are guilty sinners before God (3:9-20, 22-23), that there is but one God with one way of salvation for all men (3:29-30; 4:16-17), and that God's eternal plan involves both Jews and Gentiles (11:11-32).

4. The Human and Divine Natures of Jesus

Paul refers briefly to the human and divine natures of Jesus in 1:3-4. He does not expound on the two natures of Christ at length, because he is writing to fellow believers who know these truths. We will do well to review these truths at the beginning of our study, however, for they constitute part of the unemphasized backgrcund of Romans.

As far as his human ancestry was concerned, Jesus was a descendant of David. This fact would have been significant to the Jews. God had promised David, the second and greatest king of Israel, that one of his descendants would establish the throne of his kingdom forever. God would love David's son (descendant) so much that he would be his Father forever and the king would be God's Son (2 Sam. 7:11b-16). The Jews looked forward to the coming of this *Messiah (Christos* in the Greek, i.e., "Christ"), or *anointed king*. Anyone who claimed to be the Christ would have to be a descendant of David. Jesus met the human qualifications.

Jesus was also the divine Son of God. The term *Son of God* meant more than the Jews realized when they read prophecies referring to the Messiah as God's Son (2 Sam. 7:14; Ps. 2). They believed that God was speaking metaphorically or symbolically in such passages. In fact, he was speaking literally: Jesus is *divine* as well as human by nature. He is the eternal Son, the second person in the triune Godhead. The Jews became enraged when Jesus asserted his divine nature; they believed he was guilty of blasphemy (John 5:18-23; 8:58). But the resurrection was a powerful proof of Jesus' deity. Jesus had predicted his resurrection as a witness that he was who he had claimed to be—the Christ, the divine Son of the Father (John 2:19-22).

Both by virtue of his descent from David and by virtue of his deity, Jesus was Lord. The Greek word *kurios*, which is translated *lord*, had divine implications as well as a secular meaning in Paul's day (1 Cor.

8:5-6). Christians who were ordered to swear allegiance to Caesar as Lord knew that more was involved than accepting the political lordship of Caesar: they were being ordered to acknowledge Caesar as divine. Many Christians refused to acknowledge Caesar as Lord, because they had only one divine Lord, Jesus Christ. Their refusal brought waves of official persecution upon believers for the first two centuries of the Christian era.

5. The Righteousness of God

Verse 17 states the theme of Romans: the righteousness of God. The term *righteousness of God* refers to the righteousness that God provides in Christ for sinful mankind. It also refers to the righteousness of God's character and actions. Paul proclaims the good news that God has provided a righteousness for us who have none of our own—either by nature or by virtue of our good deeds. He also defends the justice of God's dealings with men and displays the righteousness of God's character.

In Romans, the English words *righteousness* and *justice* are translations of the same Greek word, *dikaiosune*. Similarly, the English words *just* and *righteous* are translations of the Greek *dikaios*. Sometimes a passage can be understood better by substituting *just* for *righteous* (or vice versa), or *justice* for *righteousness*.

6. "By faith from first to last" (1:17)

As the Greek is more ambiguous and less specific than the English of the NIV, translators and commentators have understood this phrase in several ways. A more literal rendering of the Greek is, "from faith to faith," as in the King James Version and the Revised Standard Version. Also, the Greek word *pistis*, translated *faith* here and almost everywhere else in Romans, might be better translated as *faithfulness* in some of those places (as it is in 3:3).

Thus, 1:17 could be translated to indicate that God in faithfulness to his covenant promise has revealed a righteousness for men, to be received by faith. We shall see that Paul is very zealous to defend the faithfulness of God in Romans (e.g., see 3:3; 11:1; 11:29).

Alternatively, as indicated by the NIV, 1:17 could mean that the Christian life begins when a sinner first puts his faith in Christ; the believer then continues to live a life of faith and trust in Christ as long as he lives.

Either interpretation expresses biblical truth. Nevertheless, the interpretation adopted by the NIV probably should be preferred here on the strength of its agreement with the phrase that follows, "the righteous will live by faith," a quotation from Habakkuk 2:4. This phrase has a double meaning. The Greek word order is, *the righteous by faith shall live.* The words *by faith* can be taken with the words that precede them to indicate that those who are righteous by faith are those who shall gain life. Alternatively, *by faith* can be taken with the words that follow to indicate that those who are righteous live their lives by trust in God. Christian faith has both a beginning aspect and a continuing one—and our righteousness in Christ is truly "by faith from first to last."

LESSON 2
Romans 1:18–2:16

1. What do we need to be saved from? (1:18, 32)

2. What is the cause of God's wrath against mankind? (1:18-21)

3. How has God revealed himself to men? Has he revealed himself to *all* men? What has he revealed of himself? (1:19-20)

4. How *ought* man to respond to God's revelation of himself? How *has* man responded? (1:21-23)

5. What has God done to punish man for rejecting him? (1:24-31)

6. Has God's giving men over to sin and depravity served to bring them to repentance? *Was it intended to do so?* (1:32)

7. Some think they will escape the condemnation falling on others. On what grounds do they deceive themselves? (2:1-4)

8. Is the expression of God's wrath against sinful mankind limited to the things mentioned in 1:24-32? What more is there to the wrath of God? (2:5)

9. How would you summarize God's principles of judgment? (2:2, 5-11)

10. On what basis will God judge those who never knew the law of Moses? (2:12-15)

11. Will Jews (or Christians) escape condemnation just because they have God's Word and agree with the law of God found in it? (2:1-3, 13)

12. How much does God know of what we do, of what we think in our hearts? (2:16)

13. Is the message of judgment a preparation for the gospel or part of the gospel? (2:16)

STUDY NOTES

1. Mankind's Need of the Gospel

Paul states the theme of Romans in 1:16-17, declaring that the gospel is God's power for salvation because the righteousness of God is revealed in the gospel. In the verses immediately following, he sets out to prove that all *need* the righteousness of God revealed in the gospel. Only when men and women realize that they are in eternal danger will the message of salvation or deliverance from this danger be received as *gospel*, i.e., good news. Only when they realize that they are in danger because of their sins will they desire righteousness. And only when they recognize that they lack any personal righteousness or means for producing a righteousness of their own will they welcome a righteousness provided for them by God. Romans 1:18–3:20, the passage under study in this lesson and the next, is devoted to proving that all of mankind are sinners— lacking all righteousness and under the just condemnation of God.

2. The Wrath of God

The gospel reveals the wrath of God as well as his righteousness. The word *wrath* (Greek: *orge*) denotes both the hot anger God feels toward sin and the sinner and also the punishment he inflicts on sinners; i.e., it denotes both the attitude and the action of God toward sin and toward those who practice it.

God's wrath has both present and future aspects. He expresses his wrath in the present age by hardening men in their depravity (1:24–31). He will express his wrath in the age to come as eternal punishment, to be unveiled on the day of judgment (2:5).

God's wrath is *revealed* (Greek: *apokaluptetai*, literally, *uncovered* or *laid bare*) from heaven. Apart from the active, gracious revelation of God, men are too blind to see that their present depravity and degradation are punishment from God (see note 4). They may attribute the sorry moral state of the human race to excessive affluence, lack of parental discipline, lenient courts, ignorance, or other human or environmental causes, but they do not recognize it as punishment inflicted by an angry God.

Men have no inkling that the day of God's final judgment is coming, unless they accept his revelation of that fact in the Bible. Men may fear some sort of worldwide catastrophe—nuclear holocaust, environmental disaster, famine or pandemic disease brought on by overpopulation—but they do not expect God to end this present age suddenly and apocalyptically with a summary, sovereign expression of his wrath toward sinners. Yet, he has declared repeatedly in his Word that he intends to do precisely that (see Ps. 2:4–5; Zeph. 2:1–3; Matt. 3:7; 2 Thess. 1:7–10; 2 Pet. 3:7).

3. Natural Revelation

The created world reveals God clearly enough that all men and women can perceive his power and divine nature and know their duty to worship him (Ps. 19:1-4; Acts 14:15-17; 17:24-28). Therefore, when they do not acknowledge and worship their Creator, they are "without excuse" (1:20). The fact that many no longer see the truth of God in the order and beauty of the natural world witnesses to the depravity of the human mind (1:28).

Paul's words in 1:18-25 describe a worldwide historical apostasy from the true God after the fall. (Let us be clear that Paul is not redefining the fall here.) Noah's descendants turned creation on its head by worshiping the things God created rather than the One who created them. In 1:23-25, Paul refers to the idol worship of his own day—something modern man finds amusing. But is scientific, rational Western man any closer to recognizing the truth of God as revealed in the created world? Many contemporary men of science, those who know nature best, deny the existence of God altogether.. Is atheism any better than idolatry? Moreover, in some intellectual circles rationalistic atheism is losing ground to *pantheism* (the belief that all life is in some sense divine). Pantheistic religions, especially Eastern religions, are gaining Western converts. And there is a noticeable trend among the environmentally aware to reverence, even to deify, the earth and life itself.

4. "God gave them over"

Three times in Romans 1 we read that "God gave them over" (verses 24, 26, 28). In giving men over to the sin and degradation described in 1:24-32, God hardens men and withholds grace from them. He does not make men evil or depraved—God forbid such a thought!—but he hardens them and leaves them in the sin they have willingly chosen for themselves.

First, Paul mentions sexual impurity in verses 24-25, associating it with idolatry. The Old Testament frequently likens idolatry to sexual impurity (e.g., Jer. 2; Ezek. 16, 23; Hos. 2). Paul goes further and asserts that idolatry and sexual impurity are associated in the same persons. Those who despise fidelity to the true God are not likely to prize fidelity to their husbands or wives, and those who degrade themselves by bowing down to the images of beasts will not scruple to defile themselves physically.

Secondly, Paul states in verses 26-27 that God gave men over to homosexual vice, a further step in degeneracy. The Old Testament condemns homosexuality in no uncertain terms (Lev. 18:22; 20:13). In the days of the republic, the Romans also despised homosexuality, thinking of it as a Greek perversion. But homosexuality had been on the increase in Rome for some time by the time Paul wrote his letter. Paul knows that the majority of men and women, sinners though they be, agreed that homosexuality is an unnatural, abhorrent perversion. His point is that sin and degeneration are progressive and that their origin lies in the conscious rejection of the true God. Today, homosexuals have begun to flaunt their perversion openly in our society. Most men and women are still shocked by open homosexuality, but they should not be surprised. Such perversion is nothing new; it appears whenever a godless society is given enough time to bring its wickedness to full fruition.

Thirdly, Paul states that God gave men over to a depraved mind (1:28). Such a mind disdains God and leads the sinner into all kinds of evil practices. Paul fully expects the average pagan to agree that the practices listed in 1:29-32 are wicked. Again, his point is that rejection of God lies at the root of all evil, social as well as personal. The Greeks and Romans had never seen much connection between religion and morality, nor do some today. Does not this failure to associate *cause* (rejection of the true God) and *effect* (evil) constitute further proof that God gave the human race over to a depraved mind?

The fact that God hardens us as punishment for our sins leads to the inescapable conclusion that, left to ourselves, we could not abandon our sins even if we wanted to do so. Of course, men and women untouched by the grace of God do not wish to do so, for God has given our race over to a mind that loves sinning. The natural mind of man loves sin so much that we enjoy the sins of others almost as much as we enjoy our own (1:32). The Romans loved the carnage of the gladiatorial circuses. Today, we vicariously enjoy the violence, greed, and sexual impurity portrayed on television and film; we even love to watch and read about murder, war, physical assault, and other sins that could claim *us* as victims some day. Whether man knows it or not, his love of sin is *nihilistic:* man seeks his own destruction.

5. Paul Gets Personal

Paul's indictment of the human race in 1:18-32 is general. In chapter 2 he gets personal. It is human nature to condemn others and excuse ourselves, but Paul will have none of it. He wants every man and woman to seek Christ, but he knows that each must first experience a *personal* sense of sin and guilt. Paul knows that many will agree with his condemnation of mankind in chapter 1. He suddenly turns on such people at the beginning of chapter 2. He warns them that they will be judged by the same standards they confess to be appropriate for judging others. Jesus taught the same truth (Matt. 7:1-2).

6. The Judgment of God

Paul states three key truths regarding the day of judgment in 2:1-16. He aims not merely to inform. Paul's intention is to show that God's principles of judgment guarantee that every man, woman, and child will be condemned apart from the mercy of Christ.

The first truth is simply that the judgment of God is bound to come sooner or later. God is patient with mankind so that all may repent and turn to him, but his patience is not without end. Eventually we must all stand before God's judgment seat. When men count on his patience as an excuse to keep on sinning, they store up even more wrath for themselves.

The second truth about the final judgment is that God shows no partiality. *Every* individual will undergo judgment, and all will be judged by the *same* standard. God will exempt no one from judgment, nor will he judge some by a lighter rule than others. This truth was resisted by Paul's fellow Jews. They believed God would deal more leniently with them, because they were God's chosen people, than with the Gentiles. Paul addresses his fellow Jews in particular in 2:16–3:19 (see Lesson 3) and cuts out from under them all grounds for self-deception.

Finally, the standard of judgment will be the law of God. He will pay each one according to what he or she has done. If a person's works are those commanded by the law, that person will be rewarded. If the works are those forbidden by the law, or if that person has not done the things the law commands to be done, he or she will suffer God's wrath. Paul adds in 2:16 that God will judge our *secrets*. He will call us to account for the hidden things of our hearts, the sins we would commit if we had the means, opportunity, or daring. Jesus taught the same truth (Matt. 5:22,28; Mark 7:20-23).

The Bible student who already knows Paul's doctrine of justification by faith without the deeds of the law (see 3:20-21) may question whether anyone actually will receive a reward for good works on the day of judgment. Is Paul writing hypothetically in 2:7 and 2:10? Not at all. Many will be rewarded for their good works. Indeed, Paul himself expects a heavenly reward for faithful service (1 Cor. 3:5-14; 2 Tim. 4:7-8).

The works that God will reward on that day are not the basis of one's salvation; rather, they are the fruit of God's work in the lives of saved sinners (Phil. 2:13). Later in Romans, Paul makes several truths clear: (1) the unconverted man cannot please God with his works, since his best actions stem from his sinful nature (8:8); (2) God saves us with the intention of working righteousness in our lives (8:3-4); and (3) the good deeds that God will reward at the final judgment are his works in us (8:29-30). Christians sometimes fail to be fully aware that *we too will stand before the judgment seat of Christ,* where our works will be judged. There we will receive rewards or suffer loss (Rom. 14:10-12; 1 Cor. 3:12-15; 4:4-5; 2 Cor. 5:9-10).

Many religious people accept the idea that God will reward their good deeds; a smaller number agree that he also will punish men for the evil they do. Such people err primarily in overestimating the quality and quantity of their good works and in grossly underestimating the number and the hatefulness of their sins in God's sight. In Romans 3 Paul will drive home the hard truth that everyone deserves condemnation for his or her works.

7. The Law of God

To be judged according to works means to have one's works compared with the works God commands and forbids in his law. As used by Paul, the term *law* (Greek: *nomos*) usually refers to the law of Moses, i.e., the Ten Commandments plus the other stipulations and ordinances God delivered to Moses for his covenant people, Israel.

The Gentiles did not possess the written law of God (Deut. 4:8). How can God judge them fairly by his law when they never knew it? This question has always been a favorite of unbelievers who would deny God's right to judge the world. Our reply must be Paul's reply: the essence of God's law is written in the hearts of all, so that all are without excuse when they sin.

Paul declares that nature shows to all men and women that God exists, that they have a duty to worship and glorify the true God, and that all men and women know the essence of what is commanded and forbidden in the Ten Commandments, or the moral law (compare 1:18-32 with Exod. 20:1-17). Men are without excuse when they sin, whether or not they have known the Scriptures. Their works will be compared with the essence of the law written in their hearts—and they will be condemned.

Possession of the written law is a great blessing. The heart of man is depraved and may repress or distort the truth of God. The conscience of man may be seared so badly that it has no feeling and ceases to warn against sin (1 Tim. 4:2). But the written law is a constant, uncorrupted statement of what God requires. Those who have it know without doubt what God commands and forbids. Even so, possession of the written law does not save. God will judge people on the basis of what they do or fail to do, not on what they know or do not know

LESSON 3
Romans 2:17–3:20

STUDY QUESTIONS

1. On what grounds did some Jews think they would obtain God's approval and escape his judgment? (2:17-27)

2. Where did such Jews go wrong in their thinking? (2:17-27)

3. In verses 1, 3, 5, and 7 of chapter 3, various objections are raised against Paul's charge that all men, Jews included, stand condemned by God. Paraphrase those objections in your own words.

4. In verses 2, 4, 6, and 8 of chapter 3, Paul answers those objections. Paraphrase his answers in your own words.

5. In 3:10-18 Paul quotes several Old Testament passages: Psalm 14:1-2; Isaiah 53:6; Psalm 5:9; Psalm 140:3; Psalm 10:7; Isaiah

59:7-8; Psalm 36:1. What is his purpose in quoting these verses?

6. What do Jews and Gentiles have in common? (3:19)

7. What does the law of Moses produce? (3:20)

STUDY NOTES

1. God's Favorites

The Jews resisted the truth that they needed salvation as much as the Gentiles (1 Cor. 1:22-23). Had not God chosen Israel to be his own special people (Deut. 7:6; 10:14-15)? Had not God given the Jews his law (Deut. 4:7-8)? And had they not received the rite of circumcision as a sign of their special relationship to God? Jesus himself had affirmed that salvation belongs to the Jews (John 4:22).

The Jews' confident belief that they were and would forever remain God's favorites was strengthened when they reflected on their history. They had often been unfaithful to the Lord; they had fallen into grievous sin and idolatry time and time again. God had punished them for their sins; he had even sent them into exile into Assyria and Babylonia. Yet he had remained faithful to his covenant promises and had restored them to their land.

By the time Paul wrote this letter Israel had forsaken their idols for good. They positively gloried in the law of Moses. They were meticulous in fulfilling the most minute precepts of the law—even giving tithes of the herbs that grew in their gardens (Matt. 22:23)! If God had loved them before, surely he loved them all the more now! Paul's fellow Jews did not fear eternal wrath; they felt no need to be saved in any spiritual sense.

As the Jews of Paul's day, many in the so-called Christian countries today view themselves as God's favorites. God has blessed the Western democracies with freedom and prosperity not enjoyed by most other nations. The Christian heritage of the Western peoples is still reflected in their political, cultural, and social institutions, and this heritage is widely acknowledged by them to be the foundation of their freedom and prosperity. Many who live in the West still consider themselves Christians, though they may know little and believe less of the gospel. As the Jews considered their circumcision to be evidence of their membership in God's people, so do many people in the Western world point to their baptism as proof that they are members of the church of God. Again, as the Jews reassured themselves that they were God's people, because they possessed his Word, so do many today consider themselves Christians because they have his Word in the Bible.

Those who live in the "Christian" West have too often viewed their blessings and their religious activity (or, at least, their religious affiliation) as proofs that they are the apple of God's eye in the modern world. As the Jews who contended with Paul, they resist the truth that every one of us *personally* is a condemned sinner in need of salvation—as much as any "godless communist" or third-world "heathen."

2. Objections and Replies

Paul seeks to shatter the complacency of his fellow Jews by reiterating the truth that they are under condemnation because they break the very law they acknowledge to be perfect and just (2:21-23). In taking this approach, Paul follows the example of Jesus when he contended with the self-righteous Pharisees (Matt. 23:1-36; Luke 11:29-52). Again and again Paul hammers home the truth that God will judge all men by the same standard: the deeds they actually do, not the deeds they merely approve (2:25-29). God does not accept men because they have joined a church, undergone a particular religious rite, or possess his Word.

In 3:1-18 Paul takes up and disposes of the few remaining objections likely to be raised by his fellow Jews. *None of these objections denies the protestor's guilt.* In each case Paul's opponent is, in one way or another, throwing himself on the mercy of the court.

If they are not to be judged more leniently than the Gentiles, the first plea is that there is no real advantage at all in being a Jew. Paul replies that the greatest advantage of the Jew is that he possesses the very words of God. But the law and the prophets do not save; they only condemn, as Paul is about to show in 3:10-20.

The second objection is that God's faithfulness requires him to pardon a member of the covenant people even if that man has not been faithful to his own covenant obligations. Paul answers that the faithfulness of God does not imply that he will not enter into judgment with his covenant people. Rather, the faithfulness of God guarantees that, whenever God and man enter into judgment, God will be found in the right and man in the wrong.

The third argument is that it would be unjust of God to punish one who has actually revealed God's glory, and the contrast between the unrighteousness of man and the righteousness of God vividly manifests God's glory. Paul replies that this argument proves too much: it lets the Gentiles off the hook, too. Gentile wickedness reveals the righteousness of God even more graphically than the unrighteousness of the Jews, yet no Jew would ever argue that God would be unjust in punishing Gentiles.

The fourth objection is basically the same as the third. Paul's imaginary opponent is running out of arguments, getting more reckless and desperate. The man whose last defense is "Let us do evil that good may result" is clutching at straws! Paul dismisses him with the observation that the justice of condemning such a one is self-evident.

3. The Testimony of Scripture

Paul's closing argument as God's prosecuting attorney is drawn from the Old Testament. He quotes a number of passages—and he could have added many more—to show the universality of sin. *None* is righteous; *none* seeks for God; *all* have turned aside out of God's way; *no one* does good. These words were addressed to Jews! God himself has declared all of *them* to be sinners. The law in which Israel gloried was actually Israel's undoing, for it proved the Jews to be sinners just as the rest of mankind (3:20).

All who today claim to accept the Bible as the Word of God should likewise confess that that Word declares all of *them* to be sinners. In the face of such divine testimony, which never ceases to be true (1 Pet. 1:25), neither Jew nor Gentile can open his mouth in further defense. All must stand naked and speechless before the judgment of God (3:19). We must believe that *everyone* is as bad as the Scriptures quoted by Paul declare. We must believe that *none of us* naturally understands or seeks for God. We must believe that *all* today are just as much under the power and domination of sin as were the men and women of Paul's day. We cannot deny that some are more wicked than others, but if we think that Paul is describing only the worst of men we miss his point entirely. Comparing one person to another, we may judge some more upright than others; but in the sight of God even the best lack any redeeming qualities whatsoever. God, who looks on the heart, declares that all are so bad that none deserves acquittal—no, not one. If we find this hard to swallow, the problem lies in our faulty, sinful viewpoint and not in the Word of God (Isa. 55:6-9, especially verses 8-9).

LESSON 4
Romans 3:21-31

STUDY QUESTIONS

1. What kind of righteousness can we have? (3:21)

2. What kind of righteousness can never be ours? (3:21)

3. How and when was the righteousness of God first made known to mankind? (3:21)

4. How has this righteousness of God been made available to mankind? (3:22)

5. How do we make this righteousness of God our own? (3:22)

6. For whom is this righteousness of God intended? (3:22-23)

7. Verses 24-25 describe God's act of providing a divine righteousness for mankind. In your own words, define these characteristics of his work for us:

   a. "Justified"

   b. "Freely"

   c. "By his grace"

   d. "Redemption"

e. "Sacrifice of atonement"

f. "Faith in his blood"

8. How did God's act of providing Jesus Christ for us demonstrate his justice? (3:25-26)

9. Paul voices several assertions about the gospel in 3:27-31 which he has already proved or will prove later. What are these assertions?

STUDY NOTES

1. "But now. . . ." (3:21)

Until the appearance of Jesus Christ the history of mankind was a hopeless story of sin, condemnation, and death. Neither Jew nor Gentile had the power to attain a righteousness worthy of God's verdict of acquittal and justification on the day of judgment. *But now*, "when the time had fully come" (Gal. 4:4), God sent his Son into the world in human flesh to provide his own righteousness for our condemned race. *In Christ* there is a righteousness of God and a hope of eternal life for mankind! From 3:21 on, Paul's message is truly *gospel*, good news.

2. "Apart from law" (3:21)

Paul has already shown that no one is acceptable to God by virtue of his obedience to the law, for all are lawbreakers, even those who do not have the written law (2:12-15, 21-25; 3:19-20). Paul now announces a righteousness for us that is not based on our personal obedience to the law, a righteousness "apart from law." This righteousness "apart from law" is the righteousness of Christ.

The phrase "apart from the law" does not mean that the righteousness of Christ was unrelated to *his* keeping of the law, only that this righteousness is not based on *our* personal obedience to the law. Christ's righteousness for us consists *precisely* in his obedience to the law, both in his living a life perfectly in agreement with the law's demands and in his dying for our sins as the law prescribes. The phrase "apart from law" refers to the way we obtain the righteousness God demands, not to what Christ did to provide that righteousness.

3. The Righteousness of God

When Paul writes of the righteousness of God in Romans, he usually means the righteousness that God has provided for man in Jesus Christ rather than the righteous character of God, i.e., his intrinsic holiness and goodness (e.g., see 1:17; 3:21-22). An exception is 3:25-26, where Paul has both God's righteousness for men and his intrinsic holiness in view. The righteousness of God for men found in Christ is not the intrinsic righteousness of Christ's divine nature but, rather, his righteous life and death for us. Romans 3:25

makes it clear that we receive by faith the work of Christ, not an attribute of his divine character.

The true nature of God's righteousness filled Martin Luther with great joy. As long as Luther had believed that the righteousness of God spoken of in Romans described God's holy character, which demands that every sin be punished, he had secretly hated God. But when he came to see that the righteousness of God in Romans describes a righteousness provided by God for him, the very righteousness he needed to merit acceptance by a holy God, Luther came to love and rejoice in God.

4. "All have sinned and fall short of the glory of God" (3:23)

The ultimate result of sin is to be forever deprived of the glorious presence of God. When Adam and Eve sinned, their fellowship with God was broken. They were driven from God's presence and deprived of eternal life (Gen. 3:23-24). The Gentile nations remained separated from God. They knowingly rejected his glory in favor of their false gods and chose moral degradation for themselves, all the time knowing that they deserved death for their choice (1:23,32). God chose Israel out of all the nations to be his own people, and he dwelt in glory in their midst (Exod. 40:34-38; 1 Kings 8:1-13). But Israel fell into sin and suffered the loss of God's glorious presence (1 Sam. 4:21; Pss. 74; 79; 80). The prospect of sharing the everlasting glory of his presence (Dan. 12:2-3; Matt. 25:31-46; Rom. 2:7,10) was forfeited by Gentile and Jew alike.

Our redemption in Christ restores the hope of sharing the glory of God (5:2, 8; 8:18-21; Col. 2:27), for Christ himself is the glory of the Father (John 1:14; 17:1-5; 22:24; Heb. 1:3), and we shall be with him (1 John 3:2).

5. Guilt, Judgment, Grace, and Sacrifice

To have a mature understanding of the gospel, the relationship between guilt, judgment, grace, and sacrifice must be perfectly clear to us.

Sin, the breaking of God's law, incurs guilt before God. That guilt brings the sentence of death, the judgment prescribed by the law (1:32). We were under the curse of the law (Gal. 3:1-14), deserving nothing but condemnation. God did not *have* to save us. He *chose* to save us out of his own grace, i.e., his good pleasure and loving favor. God could not deny his holy nature by forgiving those under the curse without carrying out the death sentence demanded by his righteous law. It was his will to redeem us, but redemption according to the law—also an expression of his perfect will—had to be based on the sacrifice of a perfect life. That perfect life was Christ's.

Christ freely chose to carry out the will of his Father to redeem us (John 10:18). He lived on earth as a man in perfect obedience to the law of God. Christ took the curse and sentence of the law upon himself when he offered his perfect life in sacrifice for us. By dying in our place, he suffered God's judgment on our behalf. Because he fulfilled the law for us in his life and, especially in his death, satisfied all God's demand on our behalf, *Christ is our righteousness* (1 Cor. 1:30; 2 Cor. 5:21). Hence, Paul's later statement that God willed his grace to reign in righteousness (5:21).

6. The Blood of Christ

Critics of the Christian faith have faulted the Bible's emphasis on the blood of Christ. They consider it a vestige of an earlier, more savage and primitive stage of religion when human and animal sacrifices were offered to appease the gods. They consider the idea that God requires blood to appease his wrath to be an unworthy concept of God.

Bases for Objections. Apart from a squeamishness on behalf of such critics, their objections are based on certain philosophical convictions:

a. It is unworthy of an infinitely loving God to punish anyone at all. An infinitely loving God would desire to change and rehabilitate people, not punish them.

b. A bloody death is too degrading and extreme a punishment for our sins, at least for the sins of most of us. Most people do not deserve such a fate for the paltry sins they have committed, and an infinite God would be big enough to forgive people their sins without demanding such a terrible price.

c. It is impossible for one man to take the punishment due another. Such an act is not morally right, and a just God could not allow it.

Replies. The Christian must maintain against all critics that the blood of Christ was a necessary and sufficient payment for our sins. In answer to the above objections we reply:

a. The rehabilitation and transformation of the sinner is not inconsistent with punishment. Indeed, unless one's sins have been expiated or wiped out by payment of the due penalty, rehabilitation is impossible. An infinitely loving God will deal with guilt, not sweep it under some celestial rug. Moreover, the God of infinite love is also infinitely holy and righteous; he cannot compromise his holiness by ignoring our guilt. Our guilt can be dealt with in only one way that does not compromise his holiness: it deserves punishment and must be punished. To deny the necessity of punishing sin is to deny God's essential holiness.

b. Those who believe that most men's sins do not merit death simply do not take sin as seriously as God does. Since, in the last analysis, all sin is an offense against the infinite God, all sin deserves the infinite penalty—eternal death. True, Christians do not believe that all sins are equally evil. Some sinners will be beaten with few stripes and some with many stripes on the day of judgment (Luke 12:47-48). Yet all eternal punishment involves the infinite penalty in hell of exclusion from the glorious presence of God.

c. Even if he himself were sinless, an ordinary man, a finite creature, could not bear the sins of others, but human nature and the Godhead were united in one person in Jesus Christ. The person of Christ is infinite by virtue of his divine nature, and he was thus capable of bearing the sins of all and atoning for them. Adam, a finite man, was representative of all men in sinning (see 5:1-21, note 4). The work of Christ, however, was greater than that of Adam (5:15) and required for its fulfillment the infinite One who was both God and man (5:15-20).

But is it morally correct for one man to suffer for another's sins? Is it right to let the truly guilty party off the hook and punish one who deserves no punishment instead? How can a holy God be satisfied with that? In reply we may ask, Can one man represent another in any action at all? If *representation*—acting on behalf of another—is possible at all, why not in payment of a penalty? We allow others to pay our debts when we cannot do so ourselves. We allow others to wage war on our behalf and to raise taxes. We allow others to carry out executions—an awesome responsibility—in our name. Why should God refuse to accept the life and death of Jesus Christ offered voluntarily on our behalf? Moreover, Christ Jesus is the God-man; the person of Christ is infinite. He is morally acceptable in all he does. He can pay any price. To deny his ability to represent us is to deny his divine attributes of infinity and holiness.

LESSON 5
Romans 4:1-12

1. To whom in particular is chapter 4 addressed? (4:1)

2. The Jews were proud of their forefather Abraham, but of what could Abraham be proud? (4:2-3)

3. What was Abraham's *spiritual* condition when he put his faith in God? (4:5; also Josh. 24:2-3)

4. How are faith and righteousness related? Is our faith equivalent to our righteousness? (4:3,5; also 3:22).

5. Paul quotes David in 4:6-8 to substantiate his argument. What is Paul's point in 4:1-8, and why is David a particularly strong witness?

6. What was Abraham's *physical* condition when he put his faith in God? (4:9-10)

7. Why does Paul call attention to the fact that Abraham was uncircumcised at the time he was justified? (4:11-12)

STUDY NOTES

1. The Justification of Abraham and David

The law was of supreme importance in Judaism, and Paul knew that most of his Jewish kinsmen did not accept the truth that they could not be justified by the works of the law. Since the Jews boasted of their descent from Abraham and gloried in the blessings promised to David, Paul emphasizes that both Abraham and David were justified exactly as he has been preaching—through faith *without* works of the law. He quotes the Old Testament in support of his case (regarding Abraham, Gen. 15:6; regarding David, Ps. 37:1-2).

2. The Significance of Circumcision

In 4:9-11 Paul tells both what was not and what was the significance of circumcision. It was *not* a sacrament bestowing God's verdict of justification. Abraham was justified before he was circumcised, while he was yet ungodly, because he believed God. Circumcision was a "sign" and "seal" of the righteousness Abraham had received simply by believing the promise of God. God's promise to Abraham constituted a *covenant* with Abraham. Circumcision was the official "sign and seal" of that covenant, much as a notarized signature is a visible sign and seal of a human agreement in our society.

God commanded that Abraham's male descendants were to be circumcised also (at eight days of age). God had made his covenant with them as well as with Abraham himself (Gen. 17:4-8). They were beneficiaries of the covenant even before they were born (Ps. 139:13-17; Isa. 49:1, 5); hence they also received the sign and seal of the covenant. Jewish parents were to bring their children up in the knowledge of the covenant promises, believing that they would come to personal faith in the God of Abraham and so be personally justified.

Circumcision bound a Jew to keep the law of God (Gal. 5:3). Obedience to the law was the condition for receiving the blessings of the covenant; disobedience brought condemnation and God's curse (Deut. 27:26; Gal. 3:10). Yet the law was given to Moses more than 400 years *after* God had made his covenant with Abraham (Gal. 3:17). Neither the obedience nor disobedience of Abraham's descendants altered Israel's status as God's covenant people. In chapter 11 (Lesson 14) Paul will resolve the apparent dilemma of God's eternal choice of Israel in spite of their sin and unbelief.

Too many Jews presumed upon the unchanging faithfulness of God in keeping his covenant with Israel. They believed that their circumcision made them God's people automatically, *ex opere operato* (by the work performed on them). They lacked Abraham's personal faith in the God who appeared to him and covenanted with him to be his God—a faith that extended to Jesus Christ himself (John 8:56)—and the same faith to which Paul now calls them.

Today, all too many people presume upon their Christian baptism in the same way the Jews of Paul's era presumed upon their circumcision. They lack the personal faith in Christ that Abraham had, yet they believe that their baptism automatically makes them part of God's people. Paul's message to us is the same as his word to the Jews. It is faith in Christ that lays hold of the righteousness of God found in him. Our baptism—whether received as an infant or as an adult—is only a visible sign and seal of the righteousness that comes by faith. Just as the Jews could have the sign without the reality, so professing Christians today can be baptized without actually having been reckoned righteous through faith in Christ. May those who have deceived themselves or been deceived in the matter of their baptism and its relationship to personal salvation heed Paul's words to those Jews who based their hope of eternal life on the false grounds of their circumcision!

LESSON 6
Romans 4:13-25

1. What did Abraham receive as a result of having the righteousness that comes through faith? (4:13)

2. What ensures us that the promise is still valid? (4:14-16)

3. How can Gentile believers in Jesus know that *they* will receive the promise made to Abraham? (4:16-17)

4. In what kind of God did Abraham believe, and what did he believe God could do? (4:17)

5. How is Abraham's faith like our own? (Compare verses 17 and 24.)

6. Compare Genesis 17:17-18 with Romans 4:19-20. How can Paul claim that Abraham did not waver through unbelief?

7. What does the death of Christ have to do with our salvation? (4:25)

8. What does the resurrection of Christ have to do with our justification? (4:25)

STUDY NOTES

1. Our Share in Abraham's Blessing

God's covenant promises to Abraham included the declaration that this man would be a father of many nations (4:17; see Gen. 17:5). Which nations could claim descent from Abraham? There were the Jews, through Abraham's son Isaac; the Arabs, through Abraham's eldest son Ishmael; the Edomites, through Isaac's son Esau; the Midianites, through Abraham's second wife, Keturah; and a handful of small, desert-dwelling tribes through unspecified concubines. These peoples, however, could hardly be described as "many nations."

The fact is that when God made his promise to Abraham, he had Abraham's spiritual descendants in view. Paul informs us in 4:16 that all who share the faith of Abraham are his children and heirs. They will constitute "a great multitude that no one could count, from every nation, tribe, people, and language" (Rev. 7:9). In Romans, Paul is neither redefining the scope of God's covenant with Abraham nor denying that God's promises apply to Abraham's physical descendants. But the Holy Spirit had shown Paul that God's promise to Abraham of a son and heir had found its true fulfillment in Jesus Christ (Gal. 3:16). Of all Abraham's descendants, only Christ was perfectly faithful to the terms of the covenant (the law) and deserving of the promised covenant blessings.

The fact that Jesus Christ is the true heir of Abraham is of great significance. Those of us who trust in Christ are *in him*. What he did, he did for us; what he received, he received for us. *In him* we are the spiritual offspring of Abraham and heirs of the promises God made to Christ (Gal. 3:26-29; Eph. 1:3-13).

2. The Circumcision of Abraham and Our Baptism

Abraham was circumcised as a sign and seal of the righteousness he had received by believing God's promises to him. Abraham circumcised his children also, even though they were too young to know or believe God's promises to them, for they were included in the promises. Generation after generation, Jewish boys were circumcised as a sign that they belonged to the covenant people and were heirs of the promises made to Abraham.

Circumcision did not confer justification *ex opere operato,* i.e., by virtue of the act performed. Every Jew had to *believe* that he was included in the people of God and was heir to God's promises (2:25-29). Although many of Abraham's descendants would fail to believe the gospel preached to Abraham, God did not command that circumcision wait upon personal faith. All Abraham's offspring were to be considered his heirs and members of the family of God until they demonstrated by unbelief that they were not his spiritual children (John 8:39, 56).

We who are in Christ are Abraham's true heirs. Rather than circumcision, we receive baptism. The visible sign of the covenant has been changed, but the spiritual meaning is the same. Our baptism, which represents our identification with Christ in his death and resurrection (Gal. 3:27), represents our circumcision in a spiritual sense (Col. 2:11-12). Baptism does not save us any more than circumcision saved the Jews. We must receive and exercise personal faith in God's promises to us in Christ.

Baptism, like circumcision, is to be administered to the children of all believers as well as to believers themselves. The covenant and promises we enjoy are the same as given to Abraham and his posterity. Although the sign of the covenant has been changed from circumcision to baptism, the promise is still "for you and your children and for all who are far off—for all whom the Lord our God will call" (Acts 2:39). Unfortunately, some baptized children will grow up to be unbelievers. But until they are able to show whether or not they have personal faith in Christ, we are to consider them heirs of the promise—and so we are to baptize them.

3. The Faith of Abraham and Our Faith

All who share the faith of Abraham are his children. Abraham's faith was not a general faith in the existence of God. Even the demons believe that God exists, and they tremble with fear (James 2:19). Neither was Abraham's faith a vague assurance that God is good. Instead, Abraham's faith had both a specific content and a personal vitality that led him to obey and glorify God. If we are to share the faith of Abraham—and no lesser faith will obtain salvation—then our faith must have the same content and commitment, producing the same obedience and praise.

Paul tells us that Abraham believed in a God "who gives life to the dead and calls things that are not as though they were" (4:17). His was not an abstract faith in a God who creates life out of inanimate matter and raises all at the resurrection on the last day. Rather, Abraham's faith was centered on God's promise that he would have a son of his own, a son whose descendants would be as many as the stars of the heavens. Abraham believed that God could give life to his aged body and to Sarah's barren womb. Later, when God commanded him to slay Isaac, the son of promise, Abraham trusted that God would raise Isaac from the dead in order to fulfill his promise. (Heb. 11:17-19). It was his belief in *this* promise that was credited to Abraham for righteousness (Gen. 15:4-6).

The Scriptures indicate that Abraham saw beyond Isaac to Christ, the true Seed or Offspring to whom the covenant promises were spoken (Gal. 3:16). Jesus tells us that Abraham rejoiced at the thought of seeing his day and actually did see that day (John 8:56).

Our faith must have the same content as Abraham's. We must rejoice in Christ and in his coming. We must believe that God raised up the true Offspring of Abraham from the dead so that we might receive the promised blessing.

Our faith must also produce obedience to the command of God. Stressing that only a faith that leads to obedient action is genuine, James cites Abraham as an example of such active faith (James 2:20-23). Paul stated in 1:17 that the Christian life begins and continues by faith, and he considered it part of his apostolic responsibility to lead Christians into the obedience that comes from faith (1:5).

Our faith must also produce praise. Abraham grew stronger in faith and glorified God (4:20). The extent to which we praise and glorify God is a measure of the strength of our faith.

4. "Raised to life for our justification" (4:25)

A new believer knows why Jesus had to die. By his death he paid the penalty for our sins. The young Christian also knows that Jesus was raised from the dead after three days. However, the recent convert is not always fully aware of what Jesus accomplished by his resurrection. Paul writes that Jesus was raised for our justification. What does this mean?

Justification is God's verdict of acquittal, the pronouncement of the Judge of all the earth that a man or woman is righteous in his sight. Until the penalty for our sins had been fully paid, God could not acquit us. If the death of Christ had not been sufficient to atone for our sins, Christ would still be in the grave—and we would still be guilty before God (1 Cor. 15:13-17).

But the death of Christ *was* a sufficient sacrifice for the sins of the world. The penalty *was* completely paid. God's righteous wrath *was* entirely propitiated. Christ finished the work God gave him to do (John 17:4; 19:30). There was no way the grave could hold him once he had finished his work of atonement (Acts 2:24). The resurrection of Christ marked the completion of his work and cleared away every obstacle to our justification.

When God raised Christ from the dead, he raised him to his own right hand, the most exalted position in heaven and earth (Eph. 1:20-22; Phil. 2:8-11; Heb. 1:3b). In glorifying the resurrected Christ, God not only bore witness to the acceptability and sufficiency of his work, but placed him over all creatures as Judge of all. The Father has committed all judgment to the Son (John 5:22). The Judge who will proclaim our justification to the universe on the last day is none other than he who purchased it with his own blood (8:33-34). Though we are justified from the moment we believe, yet the risen Christ will declare our righteousness before men and angels at the end of the age.

LESSON 7
Romans 5:1-21

STUDY QUESTIONS
1. What is the ground of our assurance that we will continue at peace with God? What is the basis of our peace with God? (5:1-2)

2. What hope does this assurance bring? (5:2; see also Dan. 12:2-3)

3. It is natural to rejoice in our hope for the future, but we can even rejoice in present suffering. Tell how suffering now produces hope for the future. (5:3-4)

4. What keeps our hope strong in spite of continued suffering? How can we be sure that we will endure through thick and thin? (5:5)

5. Summarize Paul's words of encouragement in 5:6-10.

6. Paul rejoices in three things as a result of our justification. What are those three things? (5:2-11)

7. How did the sin of Adam affect us? (5:12-19)

8. In 5:13-14 Paul offers proof for his assertion that we suffer the consequences of Adam's first sin. Summarize his argument.

9. How was Adam a "pattern" (5:14) of Christ? (5:15-19)

10. How was Christ's act of redemption greater than Adam's act of transgression? (5:15-19)

11. Why did God give Israel the law? (5:20)

STUDY NOTES

1. Peace With God

As he begins chapter 5, Paul turns from the subject of justification by faith to the results of justification. The first and most obvious result of our justification is that we are reconciled to God. From being his enemies and the objects of his wrath, we have become his friends, the objects of his special favor and care. We are at peace with God.

Peace with God, as Paul describes it, is not an inner state of tranquility and contentment. Such a state may well follow from the realization that we are no longer God's enemies, but it is not what Paul has in view here. Paul is writing about an objective state or relationship between a believer and the Lord, not a subjective feeling. Psychological states have not entered into Paul's thinking up to this point. His emphasis has been on our objective guilt as condemned sinners and our subsequent objective acquittal as justified believers in Christ. Although he turns immediately to the subject of assurance (note 2), Paul says that the basis of Christian assurance is our objective relationship with God, a state of peace that has replaced the state of estrangement, alienation, and hostility that existed between us and God before we were justified.

2. Suffering in the Life of the Christian

In 5:1-2 Paul assures us that we are at peace with God and in a state of special grace by referring to God's verdict of justification on all who trust in Christ. In verses 3-10 he invites us to be assured of our status as God's people by meditating on our sufferings and their outcome.

Suffering, especially suffering because of our identification with Christ, is an inevitable part of the Christian life (Matt. 5:12-13; Acts 14:22; 2 Tim. 3:12; 1 Pet. 1:6-7; Rev. 1:9). God has ordained suffering as a means of growing in Christian virtues and character (Heb. 12:5-13; James 1:2-3). We know that troubles and suffering do not always lead to patient endurance in the faith (Matt. 13:20-21). We know that endurance and patience do not always produce godly character; continued suffering sometimes produces bitter, hardened, hopeless survivors. Paul's argument in 5:3-5 is based precisely on the difference between the way believers and unbelievers react to suffering and trouble. God gives us proof of his abiding love by working Christian character and hope in our lives through tribulation that would wither and blight souls lacking his special love and favor.

In looking to our own character for assurance we are bound to find many traits that grieve us (and God), but Paul does not bid us dwell on such defects and besetting sins. Has our faith in God and his goodness been tested, and does it remain? Do we still possess our hope of sharing the glory of God (5:2)? These are the characteristics that ought to give us assurance. The fact that we have not given up on the Lord in spite of troubles that cause others to turn away in bitterness and unbelief proves that he has not cast us away, for faith and hope in the living God are gifts of the Holy Spirit (5:5; also 1 Cor. 13:13; Gal. 5:22).

3. "We also rejoice in God" (5:11)

Three times in this chapter Paul writes, " we rejoice" (or, if the Greek verb is understood as an imperative, "let us rejoice"). We rejoice in our hope of sharing God's glory (5:2). More than this, we rejoice in our sufferings (5:3). Even more than these, we also rejoice *in God himself* because of our justification in Christ (5:11).

The fact that God has provided Jesus Christ for our justification tells us more about God than we could ever know from his law alone. The fact that God gave his Son for our sins reveals him to be a loving, gracious God who is true to his Word (John 3:16). God's love, mercy, and patience had been shown to mankind countless times in nature, in his past and present dealings with the human race, and in his Word. But Jesus Christ revealed these aspects of God's character in so surpassing a manner that we are compelled to rejoice in God

Let us recall once more the example of Martin Luther (3:21-31, note 3). While he had thought of God solely as the holy, righteous, and all-powerful, all-knowing Judge who holds all accountable for every word and deed, Luther had secretly hated God. Only when he understood what God had done for him in Christ and believed the gospel did Luther recognize him to be loving and merciful—and rejoiced in God.

4. Adam, Our Father and Representative

In 5:12-21 Paul seeks to assure us that the work of Christ was greater in every way than the sin of Adam. In these verses he proves that the action of Adam was universal and catastrophic, bringing guilt, condemnation, death, and depravity on all his descendants and rendering them utterly helpless.

Adam did not simply bring sin and death into the world as a child brings an illness home from school and infects the whole family. He did not make all men sinners simply by introducing sin as the source of the temptations to which all succumb. Adam's role in making us all sinners was much more decisive. Like it or not, Adam acted on our behalf, representing the whole human race yet unborn. His actions were reckoned or imputed to all his descendants, i.e., to all the human race. Paul is quite clear that Adam was our representative and that his sin, guilt, and condemnation are considered ours as well.

This truth is not widely believed today. People naturally feel that it is unjust and unfair to be condemned for someone else's sin. Indeed, the Scriptures tell us that all are responsible for their own sins, not those of their fathers or sons (Ezek. 18, especially verse 20). But Adam was a special case. He was the first man, the father of us all. He was a *type* or figure of Christ in that God made him, an individual human being, the representative of the many. He acted for us all, Paul asserts. How else could we explain the universality of death, the penalty for transgressing God's law, extending even to those who did not possess the written law (5:12-24)?

We note as a practical matter that Paul in Romans 1–3 makes no reference to our condemnation in Adam. In those chapters he was not seeking so much to prove the fact of universal sin and guilt as to convert men and women. His earlier argument was based on the sins we personally commit, whether trespasses of the written law by Jews and others who possess the Scriptures or of the unwritten law in their hearts by Gentiles. Perhaps Paul felt that only those who had already been justified through faith in Christ were able to accept the truth that they were born with sin already put to their account.

Adam incurred *guilt* before God when he sinned; he also *died that very day* as God had decreed (Gen. 2:17). Since Adam lived to a ripe 930 years, his death on the day he sinned must have been a *spiritual* death. Adam's very nature became corrupt, sinful, ungodly, and depraved. He passed along this to his descendants. We inherit a sinful nature from Adam just as we inherit physical characteristics. Theologians call this inherited sinful nature *original sin*. Our inheritance from Adam consists of imputed sin and a sinful nature. Beginning at conception, before we enter this world, we are burdened down with guilt, condemnation, and corruption.

5. Romans 5:13-14

Verses 12-14 of chapter 5 have been the subject of widely different interpretations by commentators. The last clause of verse 12, "because all sinned," has been the center of marked debate. Do the words *all sinned* refer to the personal sins of all or to the identification of all with the sin of Adam?

Verse 12 begins but does not complete a comparison and contrast between Adam and Christ. (Compare verse 12 with verses 15-19, where Paul draws several comparisons and contrasts between Adam and Christ.) Verses 13 and 14 are parenthetical. Apparently, after writing "all sinned" Paul deemed it necessary to interrupt the comparison and contrast begun in verse 12. He did so because this statement ("all sinned") was likely to be disputed by some. Verses 13 and 14 are intended to prove his point in verse 12. But what is that point? And what is the logic of Paul's argument in verses 13 and 14?

Paul wishes to prove that all were constituted guilty sinners in Adam. He has already proved that all have personally sinned (1:18–3:20), but that fact might be explained by asserting that each man falls as Adam fell, by personal transgression of God's law. Paul affirms in verse 13a that sin was in the world before the law of Moses was given. Since sin is nothing more or less than transgression of God's law, such sins must have been sins against the law written in human hearts (2:14-16). Paul then states in verse 13b that sin is not counted where there is no law. Is he saying here that God does not impute personal sins against us in the absence of the written verbal law? Many commentators have thought so. Why else would Paul have referred to the one period in human history when there was no written law? Yet such a conclusion flies in the face of Paul's whole argument in chapters 1–3, to say nothing of the teaching of the rest of the Bible! Indeed, 1:32 indicates that the law written in human hearts is "God's righteous decree"—so clear a law that sins against it are, as Adam's sin, worthy of death.

Do all people have such a law in their hearts? Certainly all who are capable of hearing and understanding Paul's arguments in Romans do. But what of such exceptions as infants, the severely retarded, and the mentally ill. These constituted a large segment of those dying in Paul's day, as they have in almost all ages. Though they know not the law, yet such individuals suffer death as well as those who know right and wrong.

The *reign*, the universal sway of death over all mankind, transgressors and nontransgressors alike, must be due to a greater cause than the personal sins of those transgressing God's known law. *All die because of Adam.* He, like Christ, acted as the representative of humanity; his sin was imputed to all.

6. Grace Abounding

Paul's aim in 5:12-21 is to show that God's grace is so great that it can completely overcome sin. To reveal the greatness of God's grace, he must reveal how pervasive is sin and how helpless is the sinner without God's grace. Paul had shown the universal extent of sin in earlier chapters. *All* have sinned personally, even the Jews.

However, Paul had not proved that all were *inevitably* sinners, guilty before God and spiritually dead even before they came out of the womb. He had not proved earlier that no one *could* keep God's law, only that no one actually *did* keep it. Here in 5:12-21 he proves that no one *can* live sinlessly. All are born under condemnation and with sinful natures.

Let us not be so zealous to prove original sin and guilt to an unbeliever that we forget either Paul's emphasis on the actual sins of men in chapters 1–3 or his major emphasis in 5:12-21 on the greatness of God's grace in Christ. No matter how hopeless and helpless we are in Adam, God's grace is greater than our plight. All of the contrasts and "much more's" in these verses are intended to magnify the grace of God in Christ so that we may "rejoice in God" (5:11) and be assured all the more of our salvation. Grace is stronger than nature. Sin reigned in death, exercising complete power over all. In those to whom he has brought eternal life, God has ended the tyranny of sin. Now grace reigns (5:21).

Grace reigns *in righteousness* (5:21). God does not bestow his grace on us with a wave of his hand, overlooking our sin. The reign of sin could not be ignored; it had to be shattered. Grace established its reign only through the righteousness of Christ, and it reigns presently only in those who have received that righteousness through faith. The tyranny of sin is still a grim reality in the lives of unbelievers.

Some have interpreted 5:12-21 in terms of universal salvation. Just as all sinned and died in Adam, they argue, so all are justified and brought to life in Christ, whether they know it or not. According to this theory, evangelism is simply telling men and women that they have been saved all this time without knowing it. This theory is wrong! Paul's entire emphasis in Romans has been that we lay hold of righteousness and life *through faith in Christ*—and the apostle reiterates the necessity of faith in 5:17. The reference to "all men" receiving justification and life (5:18) must be understood with this in mind.

In one sense, Christ died for "all," i.e., "the many" (see the answer to study question 7, 5:1-21 in Appendix B). However, all of fallen mankind are not saved (Matt. 5:13-14; Acts 2:21; 1 Cor. 1:18-28). Who exactly did Christ die for? This question is taken up again in Romans 9.

II. *NEW LIFE IN CHRIST*

LESSON 8
Romans 6:1-23

STUDY QUESTIONS
1. Compare 6:1 with 5:12-21, especially 5:20-21. What is the connection between 5:12-21 and chapter 6?

2. What is our relationship, as Christians, to sin? (6:1-2)

3. What does it mean that we were baptized into Christ's death? (6:3-5)

4. What three things follow from our death with Christ? (6:4-8)

5. How could Christ, who never sinned, die to sin? (6:9-10)

6. How can we make our death to sin and our new life to God more real in our experience? (6:11-13)

7. Sin must not be our master, because we have died to sin (6:1-13). Give another reason why sin shall not be our master. (6:14)

8. What, besides law, can make us sin's slaves? (6:15-16; also Exod. 21:5-6)

9. What is the outcome of slavery to sin? (6:16)

10. How does one become free from sin and a "slave" of righteousness? (6:17-19)

11. What is the outcome of "slavery" to righteousness? (6:19-23)

STUDY NOTES

1. The Necessity of Living for God
Paul's theme in Romans 1-5 is our need for righteousness and

God's provision of a righteousness for us in Christ. The only righteousness acceptable to God is the righteousness of Christ. It is *his*
righteousness that is credited to us when we believe in him; it has
nothing to do with our own obedience to the law.

But if one is justified by faith apart from anything he or she can do,
what becomes of God's law? Paul's doctrine of justification by faith
alone scandalized Jews, even Jewish Christians. It seemed that Paul
denied the necessity of personal obedience to God's law. Some
critics even accused him of teaching that we should sin on purpose
so that good would come (3:8). Certain Jewish believers had contended that Gentile converts had to be circumcised and keep the law
of Moses to be saved (Acts 15:1-5). Paul's doctrine of justification by
faith was completely vindicated by a council of elders and apostles
in Jerusalem (Acts 15:6-29), but the question remained: What of
obedience to God's law? May Christians live as they please now that
all their sins have been imputed to Christ?

In our day a *laissez-faire* approach to Christian living all too often
results from a misunderstanding of justification by faith. Salvation
is too frequently reduced to a 10-minute process of rushing an
inquirer through "four things God wants you to know." If the
inquirer has no objections to what has been said, he or she is
persuaded to repeat a stereotyped prayer to "receive Jesus into his
(or her) heart." The new convert is then assured that he or she is
eternally secure. The demands of the Christian life are scarcely
discussed at all—not to mention true repentance and the mercy of
God! No wonder so many of our "converts" cannot be differentiated
by their fruits from unbelievers: their lifestyles are indistinguish-
able. Is the Christian life nothing more than waiting patiently for
heaven while living just as before?

Paul addresses the role of the Christian's obedience to the law in
chapters 6–8 and 12–14. We will see that he considers it absolutely
necessary to forsake sin and live for God in conformity with his
law—but not as a way to merit or to keep our salvation. Paul also
faces the fact that our obedience at best is halfhearted, faltering, and
imperfect, much as we wish it were otherwise.

2. Baptized Into Christ

It is important to know what baptism into Christ does and what it
does not mean. Baptism into Christ is commonly misunderstood.

The Roman Catholic, Anglo-Catholic, and Eastern Orthodox churches traditionally teach that baptism is the means by which God places one in Christ. They teach that baptism is necessary for salvation, except in extraordinary cases (e.g., when one has the desire for baptism but dies before he can be baptized). They interpret passages such as 6:3-4 as referring literally to the effects of water baptism, whereby the waters of baptism actually accomplish our union with Christ in his death and bestow the grace of new life *ex opere operato*, i.e., "by the work done."

The biblical doctrine of baptism, however, holds it to be a symbolic representation of our union with Christ that is accomplished by faith. We have seen that baptism superseded circumcision as the sign and seal of God's covenant with his people (4:13-25, note 2). Baptism, therefore, bears the same relationship to our faith that the circumcision of Abraham bore to his faith. Abraham was justified by faith *before* he was circumcised. Abraham circumcised his children because the promise included them also, even though they were too young to exercise personal faith. Nevertheless, they were not personally justified until they believed God and obeyed him in faith, trusting that God's promises to Abraham were for them, too. Similarly, adult Christians are justified by faith before undergoing baptism. Though we baptize our children because God's promise extends to them, too, we do not believe that they will be saved by baptism if they fail to trust in Christ.

Verse 5 in the original Greek refers to baptism as the *homoioma*, or likeness, of Christ's death. Baptism is a picture or representation of our death with Christ and our new life in him. Christ died to sin; our baptism represented identification with him in his death. Therefore, we died to sin. Paul's words about baptism in chapter 6 were intended neither to define the role of baptism in the life of the Christian nor to exhaust its symbolic content. We read elsewhere in the New Testament that baptism also represents our cleansing from sin (Acts 22:16; 1 Pet. 3:21), yet Paul does not mention this aspect of its symbolism. His intention in referring to baptism here is to reinforce the radical claim that *we* died to sin when Christ died on the cross.

3. Dead to Sin, Alive to God

What does Paul mean by the phrase "dead to sin"? What aspect of death reflects our relationship to sin now that we have been justified by faith in Christ? Paul certainly cannot mean that we are insensitive to temptation and unable to sin (as a corpse cannot sense or respond to stimuli). We know from personal experience that Christians feel temptation and are frequently overcome by it. Indeed, Paul devotes most of chapter 7 to the Christian's struggle against sin.

The aspect of death that now corresponds to our relationship to sin is *severance*, the termination of all ties, affections, and obligations. When one dies, he or she *leaves this world* and *enters a new world*. Old debts, old relationships, old bonds are completely severed and done away with. An irreversible, total breach is made between the dead and this life.

In Christ we died to sin in this radical sense. The real me, the new me, has no citizenship in this world anymore. I am alive to God now. My loyalty, allegiance, obligations, affections, relationships, and interests are all in the new world. Paul's point is that we *already* have passed over to the other side in spirit. Despite the reality of indwelling sin, we have no business letting the old, unregenerate nature prevail when it seeks to dominate our thoughts and actions. *It* was nailed to the cross in the person of Christ; *it* is not the new me created in Christ Jesus, the me with whom God now has to do (7:17; 2 Cor. 5:17; Gal. 2:19-20).

Paul had not written about our old and new natures prior to chapter 6. If we only knew Romans 1–5 (and no other New Testament writings), we might think that the old nature, being justified by faith in Christ, would enter heaven pardoned but unchanged. But in chapter 6 Paul begins to describe the life of the believer as the life of a new man, born again (or born from above) by the life-giving Holy Spirit.

4. The "old self" (6:6)

Paul uses the term "old self" (Greek: *palaios antropos*, literally, *old man*) to denote man's unregenerate nature in its completeness: body, emotions, mind, and will. He uses the terms "body of sin" (6:6) and "mortal body" (6:12) to denote essentially the same thing, the only distinction being that the "old self" was all that I amounted to before I was saved; it was the whole of me. Now that I am born again and am alive to God by faith in Christ, that old self is no longer my true self.

Although the old self died with Christ, it was not destroyed—and it shall not be destroyed until my body dies or, if Christ returns first, I am resurrected. For the Christian, the "old self" is now the "body of sin" or the "mortal body" with its evil thoughts and desires. It is part of me, yet not the real me as God sees me, for it died with Christ. The "body of sin" still lusts, disbelieves, sins, and opposes the new me, my spirit which has been born of God.

Paul frequently uses the term "sinful nature" (Greek: *sarx*) as another synonym for the "body of sin." Other translations render *sarx* as "flesh." The word *sarx* is used in a variety of ways in the New Testament, not always negative. Paul affirms that Jesus Christ possessed *sarx*, yet without sin (Eph. 2:14). The other New Testament writers also affirm that Christ was *sarx* (John 1:14; Heb. 5:7; 1 John 4:2). The NIV translators recognized that *sarx* has a variety of meanings in the New Testament and, thus, did not always render it by the same English expression.

Throughout Romans, however, Paul uses *sarx* consistently to denote unregenerate human nature, i.e., as a synonym for the "body of sin" or "old self." In the light of this, it is significant that Paul refers to the "likeness" (*homoioma*) of sinful nature (*sarx*) when he refers to Christ's coming as a man in 8:3. Christ possessed a human nature as well as a divine nature, yet it was without sin.

5. Slaves of Sin, Slaves of God

In Paul's day slavery was an institution established by law and maintained by the power of the state. Apparently, most slaves accepted their status as a given of the social order, a fact of life they had to live with, without seeking to rebel or to flee from servitude. Indeed, in hard times men would sometimes sell themselves or their children into slavery to improve their lot.

Paul describes the hold of sin over one who has not been born again by likening it to slavery. The dominion of sin is established by the law (see note 6) and maintains itself by the power of the sinful nature. We had no choice in the matter before we came to Christ; we could not stop sinning. Most of the time we were willing, even eager slaves of sin. But when we wanted to refrain from sin for whatever reason, we found we could not. How many alcoholics, how many who abuse their wives or children, how many gamblers or drug addicts wish they could stop the behavior that destroys their health, families, fortunes, and lives, but cannot! How many "good people" wish they could curb their tongues or tempers, but fail every day! Paul writes that we were freed from slavery to sin when we died with Christ. Death severs our worldly relationships, abolishing our spiritual slavery to sin. We are alive with Christ's life now. We have a new master—we are *Christ's* slaves. Remember that in 1:1 Paul identified himself as a slave (*doulos*) of Christ Jesus (see answer to study question 1, 1:1-17 in Appendix B). We are freed from the bond of slavery that holds all who are "under law" and freed from the power of the old sinful nature to dominate our thoughts and actions.

6. "Under law" (6:14)

The individual who is "under law" is obligated to obey the law under threat of condemnation and punishment. Such a person is subject to the law and legally guilty if he or she fails to conform to it. In 6:14 Paul asserts that we who trust in Christ are no longer "under law" but "under grace." As Paul will explain in chapter 7, we "died to the law" in the death of Christ. We are no longer liable to condemnation and punishment, since Christ took those things upon himself—and so we are not under the dominion of the law.

Now that we are Christ's, we certainly are not free to live contrary to God's law. The entire burden of chapter 6 is to dispel the notion that we can continue in sin, which is transgression of the law (see 4:15). Our relationship to the law is different now. We are slaves of Jesus Christ, obligated to obey him. He bought us and we are under grace, under "the law of Christ" (Gal. 6:2) and "the law of the Spirit" (Rom. 8:2). The law of Christ is the same in content as the old law, yet different and new at the same time (1 John 2:7-8). Paul deals with these matters again in Romans 8.

LESSON 9
Romans 7:1-25

1. Whom is Paul addressing in chapter 7? (7:1)

2. What breaks the binding force of a law? (7:1-3)

3. Who was once under the law? (7:4)

4. How did I die to the law? (7:4)

5. What was God's purpose in dissolving my obligation to the law—or did he not dissolve it? (7:4-6, 12)

6. Freedom from the law does not mean freedom from serving God. In what new capacity or power do Christians serve him? (7:6)

7. What does the law do in us? (7:5, 7-11)

8. Is the law the source of sin in our lives? (7:12-14)

9. Who is speaking in 7:14-24: Saul the unconverted Jew or Paul the Christian?

10. Does 7:25 summarize the best a Christian can hope for in trying to live a holy life in this world?

STUDY NOTES

1. Dead to the Law

Paul stated in 6:14 that we "are not under law, but under grace." In chapter 7 he explains *why* we are no longer under law: we "died to the law through the body of Christ." A law is binding on a man only as long as he lives. He who has died has paid his legal debt in full and can be declared free. The law no longer has anything against him.

As the example of the married woman shows (7:1-3), the death of another can release us from some legal obligations. This has happened to us. Indeed, the death of Another has released us from *all* of our obligations to the law. Our debt to the law was infinite, for our sins are committed against an infinite God. The demand of the law is eternal death, a demand none of us could ever fulfill on his or her own behalf. But the death of Christ had infinite value by virtue of his infinite person. Three days in the bonds of death fulfilled all the law's demands on all the redeemed. Those who are in Christ are *dead* to the law, no longer *under* it.

2. "The power of sin is the law"

These words, found in 1 Corinthians 15:56, express a truth expounded by Paul at length in Romans 7: the law provokes the sinful self into sinning more. Experience shows us that telling someone not to do a certain thing usually has the unintended effect of spurring that person to do what is forbidden. In this sense, sin finds opportunity in the law to bring forth all kinds of sinful conduct in me (7:8).

The law does not cause us to sin. It does not make us do anything evil that is not in entire agreement with our own sinful natures. The sinful nature seeks occasion to express itself; it wants to sin. Sin is transgression of the law (4:15; 1 John 3:4). The law provides the sinful nature with opportunities to express itself in rebellion against God by overstepping his bounds (see Ps. 2). The law irritates, provokes, and challenges the sinful nature to sin more.

3. "Alive apart from law" (7:9)

When Paul states that he was "alive apart from law," he is referring to his lack of self-consciousness as a condemned sinner. It is abundantly clear from the early chapters of Romans, as well as from other Scriptures, that we are born with sinful natures and under condemnation of death for Adam's sin imputed to us. But we do not naturally know this. We first become aware of our sin and guilt when we realize that our personal acts and thoughts are offenses against God. When we compare our conduct, thoughts, and motives with the standard of God's law, we discover ourselves to be sinners. The hearing or reading of the law causes us to realize that we are guilty before God and liable to the punishment of death. The law written in our hearts accomplishes this function (2:14-15); the written law brings our personal condition home to us with even greater impact.

Some interpreters take 7:7-11 literally. Appealing to 5:13, they maintain that one is not chargeable for sin unless he or she has broken a known law. They believe that little children are not guilty of sin until they have reached the "age of accountability." Then why do infants, the severely retarded, and any others "incapable" of personal sins (if there be any others) die? We have already seen that all are born under condemnation for the sin of Adam and are born with sinful hearts, whether they know it or not (see Rom. 5:1-21, note 4). We must conclude that Paul's words in 7:7-11 describe the birth of his *awareness* that he was a sinner and deserving of death. We shall discover that the entire seventh chapter from verse 7 on deals with Paul's self-consciousness: first as a sinner in need of justification (verses 7-13), then as a new man in Christ struggling to overcome the old sinful nature and live for God (verses 8-25).

4. The "wretched man" of Romans 7: Saul or Paul?

Verses 14-25 of chapter 7 are among the most controversial in Romans. These verses express the anguish of a man who loves the law of God but finds himself defeated as he tries to live according to that law. He is a man at war with himself, and the old sinful nature is portrayed as victorious in his life. The admission that he cannot find a way to do the good he wants to do, the tone of frustration and defeat—these features of 7:14-25 have led many capable commentators to conclude that Paul cannot be describing his experience as a Christian, but rather his former life as a sincere Jew trying to keep the law of Moses. Such commentators admit that the Christian struggles against sin, but they deny that the Christian's conflict can end in the kind of repeated failure described here. They contend that verses 14-25 are a direct continuation of verses 7-13, a section that all interpreters agree describes Paul's pre-Christian experience. Many other equally capable commentators hold that verses 14-25 reveal Paul's experience as a Christian. Saul the unconverted Jew considered himself blameless according to the law; Paul the Christian knew better (Phil. 3:4-6). As Christians, we love the law of God, desire to obey it, and feel anguish and remorse at our failures. We never loved the law or struggled against sin within us (except, perhaps, out of fear of judgment) before we came to know Christ.

Which view of verses 14-25 should we adopt? The second interpretation is preferred on both grammatical and psychological grounds, as well as on the basis of its agreement with the rest of Scripture. Grammatically, the verbs found in verses 7-13 are in the simple past tense (the Greek aorist tense), whereas those in verses 14-25 are in the present tense. Paul changed tenses for a reason. That reason can be nothing else than to indicate that verses 14-25 refer to his present experience as a Christian.

Psychologically, Paul's honesty in verses 14-25 speaks to our own experience as Christians. Here is a man who has been through the struggles I am going through as I try to live for God and forsake sin. I never felt such inner conflict before I turned to Christ. I never felt that the sin within me was *foreign* to me, "no longer I" (verses 17, 20), before I was born again.

Other Scriptures reinforce this interpretation. Compare verses 14-25 with Galatians 5:14-17. The Galatians passage is clearly parallel to these verses (as Galatians itself is parallel to Romans), and the Galatians passage clearly refers to the experience of the believer.

When all is said and done, should not the Christian have victory over sin? Is not Paul's aim in Romans 6–8 to encourage Christians to overcome sin? How can Paul's exhortations in 6:1–7:6 be effective if he is forced to confess his own failure to conquer sin in 7:14-25?

Without minimizing the force of Paul's confession in 7:14-25, we must recognize that he is not presenting the whole of his Christian experience here. Elsewhere Paul speaks of his life for Christ with more satisfaction. (See 1 Cor. 11:1; 15:10; 2 Cor. 4:2; 6:4-8; 12:2; Eph. 5:1; Phil. 1:21-22; 1 Thess. 1:10; 2 Thess. 3:7; 2 Tim. 3:10.)

Here, Paul emphasizes the defeats and failures of the Christian life to reinforce his argument that the law stirs up sin in fallen human nature—*even in the Christian*. There is a "law of sin" dwelling in the members of my body that still wars against the "law of my mind." Nevertheless, that very body can be yielded to God as an instrument of righteousness (6:13) now that I am no longer under law but under grace. Paul will expound this truth at length in Romans 8. However, taken without chapter 8, chapter 7 offers no hope of victory over sin in the Christian's life until the final resurrection, when the "body of death" (7:24) will be replaced by a spiritual body (1 Cor. 15:42-57). In chapter 8 Paul will affirm that even in this life we can—and must—overcome sin and live for God.

5. "The law of my mind" and "The law of sin" (7:23)

The word *law* (Greek: *nomos*) appears seven times in verses 21-25. *Nomos* has several meanings in this short paragraph. We will understand these verses better as we distinguish clearly between the various *laws* mentioned.

In verse 21 Paul discovers a *law* at work in his life: evil lies close at hand whenever he would do good. Here *law* has a meaning similar to our use of the word in phrases such as "law of supply and demand" and "law of gravity"; *law* describes the way things are in the world, i.e., a law of nature.

In verse 22 Paul refers to the "law of God," which means here just what it means throughout Romans. The *law* of God is his revealed will for mankind, what he commands and forbids us to do.

In verse 23 we find the word *law* three times. The first and third references are to the "law of sin" at work in the members of his body. Here *law* refers to the will of the sinful nature and what it commands; it is opposed to the will of God and what he commands. The second reference to *law* in verse 23 is to the "law of my [Paul's] mind." *The passage makes it plain that this law is none other than the "law of God"* (7:22).

Paul's fundamental point in the last paragraph of chapter 7 is this: there is a law at work in his body (expressing the will of the old sinful nature) which is at war with the law of God (expressing God's will) that rules Paul's mind. The same truth is expressed in different words in Galatians 5:17. As long as Paul remains in "this body of death" (7:24), it is inevitable—a law of nature—that evil is close at hand even when he wants to do good. So it is with us as well. Yet we can and must triumph in our struggles with sin, as Paul affirms in the next chapter.

LESSON 10
Romans 8:1-17

STUDY QUESTIONS
1. What verdict does God pass on those who belong to Christ Jesus? (8:1)

2. What do the phrases "the law of the Spirit of life" and "the law of sin and death" mean? (8:2; also 7:6, 14a)

3. How did we receive the verdict of "no condemnation"? (8:3)

4. Why was it impossible to receive such a verdict under the law? (8:3)

5. What was God's purpose in condemning sin in the body of Christ? (8:3-4)

6. How do the justified live? (8:4-5)

7. How do the justified think? (8:5-6)

8. How do the condemned think? (8:6-8)

9. What is the believer's relationship to his sinful nature (or flesh)? (8:9-12)

10. How can believers live for God in their mortal bodies, which still bear their old sinful nature? (8:13-14)

11. What does the Spirit of God do for us in our struggle against sin? (8:13-16)

12. What is our relationship to God now that we are Christians? (8:14)

13. How can we be assured that we are God's children? (8:15-16)

14. What hope does this assurance give us? (8:17)

STUDY NOTES

1. No Condemnation

Many Christians find it difficult to accept the joyous truth that there is absolutely no condemnation remaining for those who are in Christ. They are painfully aware of the struggles between their born-again spirit and the old sinful nature that still dwells in them. They find themselves continually losing the battle with the old nature. Since all Christians continue to stumble and fall into sin, on what grounds can they have any assurance that the continued presence of the old sinful nature (flesh) will not bring them into condemnation?

Seeking to assure those in Christ that they face no condemnation, Paul reminds them here that Christ came in the very likeness of sinful man to receive condemnation for their sins and to give his life as a sin offering (8:3). His human nature (flesh) was real human nature—Jesus was no phantom man—yet without sin (John 1:14; 1 John 4:12). Real human nature, Christ's human nature, suffered for their sins. There is no more condemnation in store for human nature, because human nature suffered its full punishment on the cross of Christ.

How could Christ assume human nature without assuming *sinful* human nature? Is not human nature inherently sinful? No, sinfulness is not an attribute of human nature *per se*, i.e., a necessary feature of being human. Was not Adam fully human before he sinned? True, Adam's nature suffered the corruption of sin when he fell, and all his descendants born according to the ordinary course of nature inherited his sinful human nature. But the conception of Jesus Christ was a special case. Although his mother, Mary, inherited the same sinful nature we all inherit from Adam, the conception of Christ was a miraculous event in which his holiness was preserved, as the Scriptures explicitly state (Luke 1:35). His human nature was *identical* to the sinful human nature we all have, except for the sin (8:3).

When Christ died, he bore condemnation not only for our personal sinful acts, words, and thoughts (4:25) and not only for the sin of Adam imputed to all of us (5:15-19), but also for our sinful human nature itself (8:3). There is no longer any sin or sinfulness personally committed, imputed, or indwelling for which the believer may be held liable. No more condemnation for those in Christ!

2. *"The law of the Spirit of life"* (8:2)

Paul frequently contrasts the work of the Spirit in the life of the Christian with the work of the law of Moses (see, for instance, 2 Cor. 3:6-9; Gal. 3:2-5; 4:4-7). Superficial readers of Paul frequently conclude that he thinks poorly of the law of Moses, but careful readers will reject this thesis. In fact, the content of the law of Moses and the content of the law of the Spirit are the same. Both express the holy will of God for mankind.

The difference between the written law and the law of the Spirit is this: when we have the Spirit, we have within us the knowledge, desire, incentive, and power needed to obey the will of God expressed in the written law. We read in 1 John 2:7-8 that the difference between the old and new commandments is that the new commandment is the old commandment *now coming true in our lives*. We read in Jeremiah 31:31-34 that the new covenant will no longer be an external written code, but will be written in the hearts of God's people. Yet, the covenant law is the same law of God, the same divine will for mankind, in both instances.

The written law was a "ministry that brought death" (2 Cor. 3:7). It served only to stir up our sinful nature to further rebellion and to increase our transgression and guilt. By contrast, the "law of the Spirit of life" is God's law written in our hearts, urged on us and worked out within our lives by the Spirit of God who has made us alive in Christ and now dwells within us. By the Spirit who regenerated us and gave us life we can and must triumph over our old sinful natures.

3. Sanctification

Verses 4-13 speak of the believer's sanctification. *Sanctification* is a theological word denoting the process of becoming holy in thought, word, and deed. These verses state some important truths about sanctification: (a) sanctification follows justification; (b) sanctification is the work of the Holy Spirit within us; (c) the sanctification of our thoughts precedes the sanctification of our deeds; (d) sanctification entails putting the deeds of the sinful nature to death; (e) sanctification is a necessity for the Christian; (f) there is no method or technique for attaining quick sanctification.

a. Sanctification follows justification. Verses 3-4 indicate that Christ's work for us, the basis of our justification, precedes the work of the Spirit of God in us, i.e., our sanctification. The truth that sanctification follows justification is explicitly denied by the Roman Catholic Church, which teaches that the work of the Holy Spirit within us constitutes part of the righteousness of Christ that makes us acceptable to God. Many Protestants are Roman Catholics at heart in this matter, believing that the quality of their Christian lives determines in part their acceptability to God. This error is responsible for much of the lack of assurance of salvation seen in believers.

Let us confess that there is "no condemnation" *now* for those in Christ (8:1), in spite of the fact that we are "wretched men" because we fail so often to translate our holy desires into action (7:25).

b. Sanctification is the work of God's Spirit in our lives (verses 4b, 11, 13). We do not have within us (i.e., in our human nature) the power or inclination to live for God. The Holy Spirit supplies the desire and ability to obey God when he *regenerates* us (gives us new life) and takes up residence in us.

c. The sanctification of our thoughts precedes the sanctification of our deeds (verses 5-7). Those who have the Spirit—and all genuine Christians possess the Spirit (verse 9)—think about the things of the Spirit. (The things of the Spirit are enumerated in Gal. 5:22-23 and Phil. 4:8.) The things of the Spirit are on our hearts even when we are hindered from doing them by the weakness of our sinful nature (7:14-25). Only as our minds are transformed can our actions be conformed to the will of God (12:2). We must *know* how to live rightly before we can so live; the desire to obey must precede obedience. Here, Paul relies on the principle he will enunciate in chapter 12: "be transformed by the renewing of your mind" (12:2).

d. Sanctification entails putting the deeds of the sinful nature to death. This is an active process. Although sanctification is the work of the Spirit of God within us, we are not to wait passively for the Spirit to walk us through the motions of righteousness like puppets in a show. We are actively to refuse to do what the sinful nature prompts us to do and consciously to choose, instead, to obey the law of God. Our inner man is to treat the sinful nature as if it were dead—for it really did die with Christ (Gal. 2:20)—and to refuse to have any dealings with it (8:12-13). We are not to listen to the sinful nature or to think about how to gratify its desires (13:14).

e. Sanctification is a necessity for the Christian. Paul here dispels any notion falsely derived from Romans 7 that we must resign ourselves to failure in trying to live for God, or, worse, to be satisfied with such failure! In that previous chapter he had not mentioned the Holy Spirit, the source of our power to prevail over the sinful nature, but chapter 8 is full of the Holy Spirit. No one can claim to be

a Christian who has not experienced the inner battle between the
Spirit and the old sinful nature. The true Christian continues to fight
it out until victories come (verses 12-13). We will not achieve per-
fection in this life; we will continue to stumble and fail and suffer
defeats. Nevertheless, we ought to experience victory in increasing
measure, even as we grow in awareness of how sin permeates our
lives. If we cease to fight against sin in our lives, if we lose the desire
to live in increasing obedience to the law of God, we ought to
examine ourselves to see if we truly are Christ's and really have the
Spirit of God (verses 13-14).

f. Paul does not give us a list of rules for victory in the struggle
against sin. Indeed, he furnishes no "practical" help here at all.
Sanctification cannot be reduced to a technique or method. Paul
simply states the truth of what we are and what we have in Christ,
leaving it to the Holy Spirit to give us understanding of that truth
and to show us how to apply it in our own lives. He expects that the
Holy Spirit will motivate and empower us to do what he shows us
we must do.

4. Sons and Heirs
Ask your neighbor, "Who are the children of God in this world?"
He or she is likely to reply, "*All* of us are God's children." Apparently, this belief was also common among the pagans in Paul's
day (Acts 17:28).

The Jews took a more restrictive view; only Israelites were children of God (John 8:39-41). Paul is even more limiting. In 2:25-29 he
argues that a true Jew is not one who has merely undergone physical
circumcision, but rather one whose circumcision is of the heart, one
who shows by constant, faithful obedience to the law that he is a son
of Abraham (see also Matt. 3:9-10). Christ similarly told the Jews
that everyone who commits sin is a slave of sin, not a son of God
(John 8:33-34, 41-44). Indeed, *all* who are under law find that they
are not sons of God, but slaves to sin (7:5-11).

Viewed in the light of what he wrote earlier in Romans, Paul's
statement in 8:14 is remarkable. In Christ we are no longer slaves
under law, but *sons* led by the Spirit of God. To be forgiven, yes, that
we could hope for—but to be made *sons of God!* We ought to be as
surprised by the magnitude of the grace of God as was the prodigal

son by his restoration to full sonship (Luke 15:21-24). Yet somehow we are not surprised, for the Holy Spirit moves us to address God naturally as "Father," with an intimacy that those who do not know him cannot comprehend. This spontaneous intimacy is part of the Spirit's witness to the reality of our sonship.

The Spirit also gives us confidence that we have an inheritance in heaven with Christ (Eph. 1:13-14, 18). The Spirit floods our hearts with confidence in the abiding love of God even when we experience trouble and suffering (5:3-5). Paul expands on this theme in the latter part of chapter 8.

LESSON *11*
Romans 8:17-39

1. What do Christians need to experience? Why? (8:17)

2. What is Paul's estimate of his present sufferings? (8:18)

3. What is the present state of God's creation? (8:19-21)

4. Why is creation in this state? (8:20)

5. How will creation be restored? (8:21)

6. What does the future restoration of creation mean for us now? (8:22-25)

7. What does the Spirit do for us? (8:26-27)

8. Why is this work of the Spirit necessary? (8:26)

9. God works in all things for the good of *whom?* (8:28)

10. What is God's purpose for those he has chosen? (8:29)

11. What chain of events will God use in making his people eventually to be like Christ? (8:29-30)

12. What does each of the events or stages in verses 29-30 mean?

13. When does each of the events or stages in verses 29-30 occur?

14. What are the implications of verses 28-30 for the present? (8:31-34)

15. Jesus said that many would lose their faith and fall away in times of persecution (Matt. 24:9-13). Can you reconcile that statement with 8:35-39?

STUDY NOTES

1. The Bondage of Creation
Many scientists find no purpose in nature. Some claim to find

meaning in the evolutionary process, but (to judge by their writings) the majority even of evolutionists firmly deny that one can observe any purpose at work in the natural world or demonstrate that the laws and cycles of nature have any metaphysical significance.

The Christian should not be afraid to acknowledge that there is some truth in this point of view! God subjected creation to frustration, meaninglessness, and decay as a consequence of Adam's sin. The natural world in its present state is not fulfilling the end for which God originally created it; creation is "marking time" until God restores it to what it was meant to be.

God created man to be the lord of creation under his Creator; the world was made for man, to be under man's dominion and care (Gen. 1:26-30; 2:15; Ps. 8:3-8). Once Adam sinned, God would not allow nature to remain under the dominion of fallen man (Gen. 3:17-18). We have little idea what the world was like before the fall, but God must have wrought profound changes to make it what we know today: a world that supports man only by dint of his toil, a world with no more apparent inherent meaning than fallen man himself possesses. In sentencing man to death (Gen. 3:19) God also subjected creation to decay and death.

God subjected creation to frustration and decay "in hope." He purposed to redeem man and place him once more at the head of a restored creation. On the very day that Adam and Eve fell, God promised that someday a man born of woman would crush the serpent's head (Gen. 3:15). That man is Christ Jesus, who by his obedience to God dealt Satan (the serpent) a death blow and freed mankind from sin, guilt, and death. When Christ returns to establish his kingdom in its fullness, the redeemed will be resurrected and glorified; then the earth will be freed from its bondage to frustration, meaninglessness, and decay and will enjoy the freedom of redeemed mankind, fully restored to its original state (Isa. 35; 65:17-25).

2. Adoption as Sons

Paul refers in 8:23 to "our adoption as sons, the redemption of our bodies." The Greek word translated *adoption* in verse 23 is the same word rendered *sonship* in verse 15. That word, *huiothesia*, can mean adoption; it can also refer to the act of granting the full rights and responsibilities of adult sonship to a minor, i.e., a child's legal coming of age. Paul uses *huiothesia* in the latter sense in verse 15. While we are clothed with our present mortal body, the "body of death" (7:24), we cannot enjoy our full inheritance as co-heirs with Christ (8:17). We will receive all the powers and benefits that pertain to us as sons of God when our bodies are resurrected and glorified at the coming of the Lord (1 John 3:2).

Yet we are sons of God from the time we put our faith in Christ and are born again (John 1:12). The Holy Spirit is called "the Spirit of sonship" (*huiothesia*) in 8:15, because he witnesses to our born-again spirits that we are even now the children of God (8:16) and because possession of the Spirit is itself a privilege of God's children (8:9, 14; John 14:16-17). The Spirit is the "deposit guaranteeing our inheritance until the redemption of those who are God's possession" (Eph. 1:14). Because we possess the Spirit of God, we know that someday we shall enter into all the rights, powers, and splendor of mature sons of God.

3. Foreknowledge, Predestination, Calling, Justification, Glorification

Paul assures the Christians in Rome—who may already have endured persecution for their faith—that God works in all the events of our lives to achieve his purpose of making us like Christ (8:28). To prove that God is in total control and actively at work in our lives, Paul enumerates the great acts of God for us from before the world began to the consummation of all things.

God chose his people before the world began. God's *foreknowledge* is his choice or *election* of particular men and women to be his own people (Jer. 1:5; Amos 3:2; 1 Pet. 1:2). Some would define foreknowledge as knowing what will happen in advance. In this view, God's foreknowledge of persons is simply his prior knowledge of who will respond in faith to the word of Christ. Such a view of God's foreknowledge is greatly defective, betraying a concept of God that does not do justice to his sovereignty. After all, God knit us together in our mothers' wombs and ordained all our days (Ps. 139:13, 16). If foreknowledge were only prior knowledge, then ultimately the choice to believe or disbelieve would be man's; yet the Scriptures make clear that God is in complete control of *all* that comes to pass. If God knows that something will come to pass, it is because he purposes that it shall come to pass. Paul discusses election at length in chapter 9. (A full discussion of the important questions and usual objections to this biblical doctrine is found in the next lesson.) It is enough for now to recognize that God chose some to be his own people before the foundation of the world (Eph. 1:4).

God carries out his purposes without fail. He is never frustrated in achieving his aims; he is in total control. He *predestined* or determined beforehand what would occur in the lives of his elect to accomplish his purpose in and for them. Things do not "just happen" to believers apart from God's plan. Good fortune, success; suffering, trials, setbacks, tragedies, and hardships as well as seemingly random, haphazard, chance, meaningless events—all are predestined by God. Men and women deceive themselves when they think that the choices they make in life, because they are real choices from their point of view, can circumvent God's purpose for them. No matter how "freely" men choose their own paths, at the end of time they will have to look back and acknowledge that they were carrying out God's plan all along. As this is true even for unbelievers (Ps. 76:10; Isa. 45:1; Acts 2:23), how much more for those whom God has chosen for his own!

In his own good time God *calls* his elect to faith in Christ. Calling includes everything God does to bring a sinner from ignorance, complacency, and unbelief to faith in Christ. This involves the awakening of fear and concern for one's soul (Job 28:28; Ps. 86:11; Acts 16:29-30), the instilling of a sense of sin and guilt and the certainty of judgment (John 16:7-11), the kindling of remorse and repentance (Acts 5:31; 11:18), the provision of instruction and the granting of understanding regarding the person and work of Christ (John 6:42-45; 1 Cor. 1:24), and the bestowal of faith in Christ as Savior and Lord (Ps. 80:18; 1 Cor. 12:3; Eph. 2:8-9). Calling is the work of the Holy Spirit (1 Cor. 2:4-5; 1 Thess. 1:5-6).

Justification is God's act as the righteous Judge of all in acquitting the guilty sinner and declaring him just and upright before the law on the basis of the work of Jesus Christ done on his behalf (3:21-31).

Glorification is the last stage in the life of God's elect that Paul mentions here. Glorification is becoming like Christ; it entails the complete sanctification of our persons when the "body of death" (7:24) with its sinful nature is destroyed and we are clothed with a new spiritual body (1 Cor. 15:42-55). Paul has devoted a major part of chapters 6–8 to the subject of sanctification, and it may seem

puzzling that he does not mention sanctification here, after justification and before glorification. However, since sanctification is the
process of becoming holy in thought, word, and deed, what is that
but becoming like Christ?

Our sanctification is the beginning of our glorification. To the
extent that we are sanctified in this life by putting to death the deeds
of the body, so far are we glorified in this life (2 Cor. 3:18). By the
power of the Holy Spirit given to us we can put to death the deeds of
the sinful nature (8:13) and make a beginning in sanctification/glori-
fication in this life. Paul writes elsewhere of the gift of the Spirit as
the "deposit guaranteeing our inheritance" until our final redemption, resurrection, and complete glorification at the coming of Christ
(Eph. 1:14).

Glorification also encompasses our coming into the full inheritance as co-heirs with Christ, our "adoption as sons" (note 2). Our
sanctification/glorification is not completed in this life; complete
glorification awaits the resurrection of the body. Yet Paul writes of it
in the aorist tense, normally translated (as in 8:30) as a simple past
tense. The outcome is so certain that he can view our glorification as
already accomplished. God's purpose is that believers be fully conformed to the image of his Son (8:29), and his purpose must be
accomplished. Our glorification—our being made like Christ in
holiness, power, and splendor—is firmly settled in heaven.

4. The Last Word in Assurance

Paul sums up chapters 1-8 with one of the most lyrical passages in
the New Testament. Verses 31-39 bring the first half of Romans to a
close. Paul began his letter with the *wrath* of God revealed *against all
men* (1:18); he concludes the first half with the *love* of God *for his elect*.

If God is for us, who can be against us? Yes, we must face God's
judgment (2 Cor. 4:10), but the Judge is the very One who loved us
enough to die for us. As if that were not enough, the Judge is also the
Counsel for the defense, he who pleads our case (1 John 2:1). Yes,
we may suffer and even die for our faith. Satan hates our Lord and
his people, and this world is no friend to grace—but the love God
has already demonstrated in sending Christ to die speaks even more
powerfully than the hatred of the enemy. Even in our greatest
distresses, God is at work for our good, to conform us to Christ
(Phil. 3:10).

The last word in assurance to God's children is this: *God is for us!* From his choice of us before the world began, through Christ's death for us while we were yet his enemies, through his gift of the Holy Spirit to call us to Christ and assure us of our salvation and help us pray in our weakness—in all these things God shows that he is for us. After meditating on these things, how can we doubt that he will keep us in the faith of Christ and bring us to glory!

III. GOD'S DEALINGS WITH MANKIND AND PLAN OF SALVATION FOR HIS PEOPLE

LESSON 12
Romans 9:1-29

STUDY QUESTIONS

1. What is Paul's attitude toward the Jews? (9:1-3)

2. What blessings had God given the Jews? (9:4-5)

3. Why might someone think that "God's word had failed"? (9:6)

4. How does Paul answer the charge that God was not true to his word? (9:6-13)

5. What are God's criteria for choosing and blessing someone? (9:14-16)

6. What does this passage say about a man's will? (9:16-18)

7. What objections are raised to Paul's conclusions? (9:19)

8. How does Paul answer those objections? (9:20-21)

9. What ends has God destined or prepared people to serve? (9:22-23)

10. Do both ends show forth the power and glory of God? If so, how?

11. Why hasn't God already executed judgment on the "objects of his wrath"? (9:22-23)

12. Whom did God choose to be the "objects of his mercy"? (9:23-26)

13. Considering that only a few Jews turned to Christ, are we to think of God as hard in electing only a few or as merciful in electing some? Or is there some other way to view the fact that God has elected but a remnant of Israel? (9:27-29)

STUDY NOTES

1. God's Word Has Not Failed

The change in mood and subject matter from chapter 8 to chapter 9 is striking. Paul assures Christians in chapter 8 that God is for us no matter how bleak things may seem, that the God who chose us and saved us will most certainly keep us in his love forever. Chapter 8 is a message of assurance, hope, and joy. In contrast, chapter 9 begins with Paul's personal anguish over his people's rejection of their Messiah. By rejecting Christ the Jews forfeited all the blessings God had given them: their status as sons of God; his glorious presence among them; his gracious covenant with them; the law he had given them alone; the worship ordinances he had prescribed so they could draw near to God; the promises of prosperity, peace, national greatness, and worldwide dominion; and the privilege of being counted as true heirs of Abraham, Isaac, and Jacob. The Jews abandoned all these blessings when they rejected Jesus as Messiah (Matt. 23:13, 37-39), for these blessings find their fulfillment only in Christ (Gal. 3:16, 29).

Even more troubling to Paul than the lost state of his people was the suggestion that their rejection of Christ and God's consequent rejection of the Jews rendered God unfaithful to his word. It appeared that God had painted himself into a corner! Had he put himself in the position of having to renege his promises to the patriarchs by making faith in Christ necessary for sharing in the promised blessings? Can man's lack of faith nullify the faithfulness of God (Rom. 3:3)? Does man have the power to frustrate God's plan by refusing to participate in it?

These issues were so important to Paul that he devotes chapters 9, 10, and 11 to their resolution. He first affirms that God's promise will be fulfilled to those to whom it was actually made—the elect of all nations (9:6-29). He then reaffirms the necessity of faith in Jesus as the Christ as God's way of salvation for all nations (9:30–10:17); no one, not even the Jew, can be saved apart from faith in Christ. Finally, Paul shows that Israel's present unbelief is part of God's plan for the salvation of all nations, Gentiles as well as Jews, and he asserts that "all Israel will be saved" when God's plan for the world finds its fulfillment (10:18–11:36).

2. Election and the Sovereignty of God

Paul defends the faithfulness of God by affirming that not all who are Israelites by natural descent are true heirs of Abraham. God has chosen some, Gentiles as well as Jews, to receive the blessings promised to Abraham, and he has passed by the rest of mankind. Those whom he has chosen he predestines, calls, justifies, and glorifies (see 8:17-39, note 3). They are the true Israel of God (Gal. 6:14-16; Phil. 3:3), and God is faithful in keeping the promises he made to them. Since the rest of Abraham's natural descendants were never included within the scope of God's promises to him, God cannot be deemed unfaithful for not calling, justifying, and glorifying them.

Paul knows how strongly most people object to the idea that God has chosen some as his own and not others. Would not God be unjust to favor some of sinful mankind above others? Did not Paul himself affirm that God is no respecter of persons and that he judges all by the same standard (2:6-16)? Did he not conclude that none is righteous, that all are sinners, and that none will have a word to offer on his own behalf before the judgment seat of Christ (3:9-20)? On what basis can a just and loving God choose to grant repentance and faith to some and not to others?

Paul's answer is that God exercises *sovereign grace*. He has mercy on whomever he chooses to have mercy. His choice depends entirely on his will, for there are no forces or influences outside of himself making or even predisposing him to choose one above another or to choose all, many, few, or none. No one deserves his grace; no one has a claim to his compassion. God did not elect the worthy, for none are worthy. He did not elect anyone on the grounds of foreseen future faith or spiritual potential; faith is his gift (Eph. 2:8-9) and sanctification his work (Phil. 1:6; 2:13). When God chose some to be his people before the world was created he selected them to carry out his own purpose—and for no other reason.

And what is God's purpose, according to which he elected some and not others? The overall purpose and plan of God in this world is to reveal his own glory, wisdom, and power (9:17, 22-23; Eph. 3:9-11; Heb. 6:13-18). He appoints men and women to different ends for that purpose. He reveals his holiness and wrath against sin by judging the evildoer (9:22; Prov. 16:4); he reveals his love by having mercy on other undeserving sinners (9:23; also 5:8). He reveals his absolute freedom of choice and the absolute depravity and helplessness of mankind by favoring those who are not wise or powerful or good according to the standards of this world (Luke 5:30-32; 1 Cor. 1:21-31).

For another common objection to election and its refutation, see note 5.

3. Election and the Love of God

If we are willing to face the facts with an open mind, we must accept election as a fact. What Christian would deny that *God* brought him or her to repentance and faith in Christ? Who would dare deny that, if *God* had not awakened us, we would still be living in unbelief and under the just condemnation of God for our sins? And what Christians would deny that many men and women who go to their graves unrepentant and unbelieving, lost forever, are no worse—perhaps even better—than we were before God spoke to our hearts and kindled faith within? It is a *fact* that all who are saved are chosen by God, and it is also a *fact* that some are not saved. We have no choice but to conclude with Paul that God elected some undeserving sinners to eternal life and appointed others, no worse, to suffer justly the wrath their sins deserve.

Many earnest Christians are not satisfied with the doctrine of election. They may admit that God has the right to exercise sovereign grace, but they find it hard to admit that he actually does so. If salvation is ultimately a matter of God's choice rather than man's choice, must we conclude that God's love is limited because all are not saved? Let men be lost because of their own choice, because they refuse God's grace, but never because God did not love them enough to want to save them! When faced with reconciling the unbelief of some with the unlimited power of God to save, foes of the doctrine of election frequently declare it a mystery that man will never solve.

While those who contend for the doctrine of election also admit that they do not have all the answers, they maintain that that is no reason for denying a truth that the Scriptures plainly teach and Christian experience so positively confirms. They contend that the doctrine of election is entirely consistent with the love of God for all the world. We shall see that Paul is of the same opinion. We must patiently wait while he develops his argument and brings it to a conclusion in chapter 11. There he will affirm that the purpose of God in election will ultimately flower in the salvation of a great multitude of both Jews and Gentiles (Rev. 7:9). Paul does not teach that every individual sinner will be saved, but he shows that the working out of God's purpose in election brings about the salvation of an innumerable host in Christ drawn from every land and people (John 12:32; Eph. 1:9-10; Phil. 2:9-11; Rev. 15:4).

4. Hard Sayings

Verses 13, 17, and 22 contain statements that give people great offense. Even Christians, who love and accept the Bible as God's Word, may find it difficult to reconcile the all-too-clear meaning of these statements with the loving character of God revealed elsewhere in the Scriptures. Paul, whose vision of the love of God for all, Jews and Gentiles alike, is unequalled, had no difficulty reconciling the truths contained in these verses with God's love. Let us examine them and see whether we, too, can understand them in a manner that is both straightforward and consistent with the loving, holy character of God.

a. "Jacob I loved, but Esau I hated" (verse 13). We may not soften this verse by claiming that *hated* is a comparative term equiva-

lent to *loved less*. While *hate*, when applied to God, does not connote
the passions and feelings characteristic of man's hatred, it certainly
means more than the absence of positive love. Paul is quoting
Malachi 1:3 here. When we read the context, Malachi 1:2-5, we see
that God's hatred for Esau was expressed as divine judgment on the
nation of Edom, the descendants of Esau, for its sins. God hates evil
and expresses that hatred in judgment. Edom was a wicked nation
and deserved everything the Lord inflicted on it. God's love for
Jacob (i.e., Israel) was expressed in his merciful restoration of Israel—
in spite of its sins, which were every bit as bad as those of Edom
(compare Amos 1:11-12 with Amos 2:4-8). The hatred of God is
always well deserved, while his love is never deserved but wholly of
grace.

b. "For the Scripture says to Pharaoh: 'I raised you up for this
very purpose, that I might display my power in you and that my
name might be proclaimed in all the earth.' Therefore . . . he hardens
whom he wants to harden" (verses 17-18). Paul could have expressed
himself even more strongly here, for in Exodus 7:3-5 God states that
he would glorify himself in the liberation of Israel from Egypt by first
hardening the heart of Pharaoh so that he would not let them go.
God hardens hearts? Yes, God hardens hearts, as both the Old
Testament (Isa. 6:9-10) and the Lord Jesus himself (Matt. 13:13-15)
affirm.

If God hardens hearts, then how can an unrepentant sinner be
held accountable for his or her unbelief? The sinner could not turn to
God even if he or she wanted to! Let us bear in mind that when God
hardens hearts he does so judicially, as punishment for sins. Paul
made just this point early in Romans (1:28-32). While hardening
Pharaoh's heart was God's means of glorifying himself more fully in
Israel's redemption, that hardening was well deserved. In hardening Pharaoh's heart, moreover, God did nothing to Pharaoh that
Pharaoh did not willingly concur in. Indeed, Pharaoh hardened his
own heart (Exod. 8:15, 32; 9:34-35).

c. "The objects of his wrath—prepared for destruction (verse
22). Taken in context (9:20-23), this verse suggests that God made
some for the express purpose of showing his wrath and that this was
his intention for them from the very beginning. This is surely the

hardest saying of all! To be sure, Paul phrases the proposition
hypothetically: "What if God . . . ?" Yet it seems impossible to
escape the conclusion that these men and women never had a
chance. God intended from before the creation of the world that
they should show forth his glory by suffering wrath and destruction
for their sins. If the "objects of his mercy" were elect before the
creation of the world (Eph. 1:4), God also must have made his
decision regarding the *reprobate* (those he passed by) before the
world was created. Is not this a most difficult doctrine to accept?

We must not deny the implications of this verse, but we should
bear in mind that the "objects of his wrath" *get what they deserve.*
They are in fact the same mocking sinners described in 1:18-32, who
know that God exists, *know* that their deeds are evil, and "know
God's righteous decree that those who do such things deserve death
[but] not only continue to do these very things but also approve of
those who practice them" (1:32). Paul is not writing here of ignorant
or unwilling sinners! In 9:22 we see unrepentant sinners in the light
of God's sovereignty and purpose; in 1:18–3:20 we saw them in the
light of their inexcusable sin and justifiable condemnation. In 9:23
Christians see themselves in the light of God's sovereignty and
purpose—but we must admit that we are described in 1:18-32 every
bit as much as the reprobate. The phrases "prepared for destruction" (verse 22) and "prepared for glory" (verse 23) describe men
not according to their natures but according to the ends to which
God has appointed them.

And if "prepared for destruction" and "prepared for glory" describe people as God sees them and not as we see them, we ought
not to dwell too much on election except to glorify God for his mercy
and sovereign grace. We can never know who among those we
encounter in life are "objects of mercy" and who are "objects of
wrath." We are commanded to preach the gospel to every creature
in the hope that God will grant those we address repentance and
faith and in the confidence that none of his "objects of mercy" will
fail to obtain the grace of God.

5. Is Election Unto Service or Unto Salvation?

Some commentators view God's choice of Israel very differently
from the interpretation presented here. They contend that Israel
was elect of God unto service, not unto salvation. In their view God

chose Israel to carry out his work in the world: to be his witness to the nations, to execute his judgment on the earth, to bring justice and prosperity to the peoples, and to make God known throughout all the lands. God set the people of Israel apart from the other nations to be his servant to them. This, they claim, is what election is about—not predestining some to be saved and leaving the rest of mankind to perish in their sins.

There is plenty of Scripture to back up the contention that God chose Israel to be his servant. Isaiah bears especially rich testimony to this truth (to begin with, see 41:8-10; 42:1-7; 43:10; 44:1-5, 21; 45:4-6). But the Lord's choice of Israel to be his servant is not the election Paul is affirming in Romans 9, as can be seen from the following considerations:

a. Paul makes a distinction within Israel between the natural children and the children of promise (verse 8). Only the latter are the elect, and they are but a small remnant (verse 27) of the whole people.

b. The election in view in chapter 9 has as its purpose the manifestation of God's glory in his showing mercy to the elect rather than in the service of the elect (verses 16-18, 23).

c. The elect include Gentiles as well as Jews (verse 24).

d. The theory that the election here spoken of is Israel's election unto service actually supports the charge to which Paul is responding in chapters 9-11, i.e., the suggestion that Israel's unbelief renders God unfaithful to his word. If God had declared Israel to be his servant for the purpose of bringing his blessings to the whole world, what does Israel's unfaithfulness do to the word and purpose of God? Did he make a poor choice in the election of Israel as his servant?

The fact of the matter is that the true Servant of God is not the whole nation of Israel, but Jesus Christ (Zech. 3:8; Matt. 20:28; John 10:11-14; Acts 3:26; 4:27). The servant passages in Isaiah become increasingly personal and individual. In Isaiah 49:5-6 we read that the Servant is not the nation Israel but an individual who will redeem both Israel and the Gentile nations; in Isaiah 52:13–53:12 we see that the Servant suffers and dies as an offering for the sins of the many. The elect Servant is not the entire people of Israel; he is the one and only descendant of Abraham who proved true to the covenant by his perfect obedience to the law of God—Jesus Christ.

The identification of Jesus Christ as the elect Servant of God for the blessing of the nations is a precious truth, but it is not the subject of Romans 9. The election Paul has in mind is God's choice of some to be heirs of salvation according to his sovereign, gracious will. Romans 9 is clear in its meaning when taken in its natural, unforced sense. That meaning should not be distorted or denied because the natural mind of man (the "old self" of the Christian) rebels against it.

LESSON 13
Romans 9:30–10:21

1. The Jews sought righteousness, but most of them failed to obtain it. Why? (9:30–10:3)

2. Has Paul written off Israel? Has he consigned them to the wrath of God? (10:1)

3. What human action is involved in discovering and appropriating God's way of being justified? (10:4-10)

4. How can an individual make sure that he or she is one of the elect, one of those whom God has called to be an "object of mercy"? (10:9-12)

5. What prevents people from calling on the Lord? (10:14-17)

6. What can we do to awaken faith in Christ within the unconverted? (10:17)

7. Can anyone plead ignorance as an excuse for not responding to the gospel? Explain. (10:18)

8. What was Israel's attitude toward the gospel and toward the fact that the Gentiles had accepted it? (10:19-21)

STUDY NOTES

1. Righteousness by Faith: A Stumbling Stone

Earlier in chapter 9 Paul explained Israel's failure to accept Jesus as Messiah from the perspective of God's eternal *purpose*. Only part of Israel was truly Israel (9:6); only a remnant of the people were elect. Now, in 9:30–10:21 he explains Israel's rejection of Christ from a different perspective, i.e., as the *means* God ordained for the salvation of men and women. Paul's Jewish kinsmen stubbornly refused to accept God's righteousness in Christ, a righteousness received by faith. Instead, they insisted on pursuing a righteousness they could call their own, a righteousness based on works of the law.

In 10:3 Paul attributes Israel's quest for a righteousness based on the law to their ignorance, but in 10:16-21 he states that this ignorance was willful. The Jews had reason to know that they could not attain a righteousness pleasing to God by keeping the law. Nevertheless, they refused to submit to God's way of righteousness. Righteousness in Christ was—and remains—a "stumbling stone" to Jews (9:32).

The Jews had every reason to know that their privileges and standing with God as his own people (9:4-5) were entirely due to his grace and mercy. The history of Israel was one of continual redemption from oppression brought on by the people's sins. Although reward or punishment was contingent on obedience or disobedience to God's law (Lev. 26:3-39; Deut. 28), Israel's status as God's elect covenant people was not contingent on their actions. Rather, it was based on the free, loving choice of the Lord of all the earth (Exod. 34:6-7; Lev. 26:40-45; Deut. 4:25-40; 5:12-19; 7:6-16).

Faith in the promises of God has been the means by which God's elect have laid hold of forgiveness and of God's own righteousness ever since God first called Abraham out of idolatry in Mesopotamia (Gen. 12:1-4; 15:1-6; Gal. 3:6-9). God gave the law to Israel 430 years *after* Abraham and only *after* he graciously redeemed them from slavery in Egypt. He gave Israel the law as a constant reminder of their need for his righteousness (Gal. 3:17-19). God promised forgiveness to the transgressor who offered the sacrifices required by the law (Lev. 4:1–6:7; 16:1-34) in a spirit of repentance and faith (Ps. 51:1-9). The sacrifices and feasts prescribed by the law spoke clearly of the Messiah to come (Heb. 8:3-6; 9:1-28). God's people were *never* supposed to view the law as a means of establishing their own righteousness. The law was intended to show Israel how the Lord's redeemed covenant people were to serve their Savior, to make them know their own sinfulness, and to offer them forgiveness in sacrifices that were *types* or figures of the One to come.

We may think it natural that the Jews would consider their obedience to be their righteousness. The Scriptures sometimes speak that way (Lev. 18; Neh. 9:29; Ezek. 20:11, 21). But sinful human nature finds its strength in the law and works all kinds of sin in our lives (7:7-24; also 1 Cor. 15:56). The spiritually honest Jew knew that he or she was a sinner and was thus driven to plead the mercy of God promised in the law (Ps. 51:1-9; Isa. 6:5-7). For the Jews to persist in seeking their own righteousness by works of the law was pride, stubbornness, and willful ignorance.

Our Gentile unbelieving friends, neighbors, and relations are no different in their obstinacy than the Jews of Paul's day. We were the same before we came to Christ. We all found our righteousness in our own good works, and we all ignored the manifest evidence of our inherent, irreformable sinfulness and corruption, until God called us through the message of the gospel.

2. Believing and Confessing Christ

"It doesn't matter what you believe as long as you're sincere." Astonished, unbelieving multitudes will enter hell with that lie on their lips. The truth is that the faith that saves has a specific content and a definite object. In 10:5-13 Paul reiterates the content of the faith that saves. It is faith in Jesus Christ as God come in the flesh, as the One God raised from the dead when he had finished his work of redemption, as the One who proved himself to be the Lord, our God and our master. This faith is the same faith that saved God's people in ancient times, as Paul proves from Deuteronomy 30:11-14 (see the answer to study question 3, 9:30–10:21 in Appendix B).

The faith that saves is also a faith that is confessed before men. Deuteronomy 30:11-14 refers to the word of salvation as being on the lips of God's people as well as in their hearts. Paul does not pass over this point: we are saved by *believing* and *confessing* Jesus Christ. Up to this point he has stressed faith in Christ. Now he seems to add a new element, verbal confession, as another requirement for salvation. Does this additional element contradict Paul's earlier emphasis on faith alone?

When Paul insists that "it is with your mouth that you confess and are saved" (10:10b), he asserts no more than the Lord Jesus himself had stated (Matt. 10:32-33; Mark 8:38; Luke 9:26). True faith and trust in Christ cannot be hidden (Matt. 5:11-16). Genuine saving faith will confess Christ, just as genuine saving faith will gladly be baptized (Acts 2:38), love its brother (1 John 2:9-10), hate the world

(1 John 2:15), and be separate from a life of sin (1 John 3:6). The same Holy Spirit who kindles faith in our hearts moves us to confess Christ as Lord (1 Cor. 12:3; 1 John 4:2-3).

3. "Faith comes from hearing" (10:17)

How can we get someone to believe the gospel? Most of us have loved ones and friends who do not have faith in Christ. We would compel them to believe the gospel if only we could—but how? What creates faith in Christ?

Paul states that the source of faith in the gospel message is the hearing of that message itself (10:17). The Word of Christ is self-authenticating: the Holy Spirit works conviction in the hearts of the elect as they hear the message. The Word of God is called the sword of the Spirit (Eph. 6:17), for it pierces our hearts and shows us our true selves (Heb. 4:12). More than that, the Holy Spirit uses the Word as the means of grace to create faith in Christ in the sinner's heart and to increase the faith of the believer.

We do well to argue for the truth of the Scriptures, to advance the best arguments we can muster for the inspiration, inerrancy, and authority of the Bible in seeking to convince others of the validity of its message. Yet in the last analysis, the Holy Spirit speaking through the Word itself convinces and convicts hearts. Our primary responsibility is to proclaim the Word. We are to plant and water the seed (1 Cor. 3:6-7), leaving it to God to make the seed grow by its own power (Mark 4:1-20, especially verses 14 and 26-27). Even if we cannot answer all the questions and objections thrown up to us, we are to speak the Word of Christ anyway. That Word gets in among men in spite of their most careful defenses and works faith in their hearts. *It is Christ himself who speaks through the Word.* The Greek of 10:14 could be translated, "And how can they believe in the one whom they have not heard?"

4. "Did they not hear?" (10:18)

In 10:18 Paul seems to say that the whole world had heard the gospel message by the time of his writing. We know that this cannot have been his meaning, for it was his goal to preach the gospel where Christ had never been proclaimed (15:20), and he believed that he had much work yet to do (15:24ff.). What does the apostle mean, then, in 10:18?

Paul is *not* referring to the fact that the whole world has some knowledge of God through natural revelation. It is true enough that the witness of nature and of conscience leaves all men without excuse (see 1:18–2:16, notes 3 and 7). The fact that Paul quotes Psalm 19:4 here might seem to confirm the view that he has natural revelation in mind, since Psalm 19:1-4 celebrates the revelation of God in nature. We must, nevertheless, reject this interpretation. Paul has been writing of faith in Jesus Christ as Savior and Lord—of saving faith. Natural revelation does not reveal Jesus as God come down from heaven, God made flesh and crucified for our sins, the risen Lord.

Paul's reference in 10:18 is to the Jews. We must bear in mind that chapters 9, 10, and 11 are concerned with Israel's unbelief. Let us note that verses 18 and 19 are parallel rhetorical questions. Verse 19 refers to Israel; verse 18 must also refer to Israel. The phrases "all the earth" and "the ends of the world" in 10:18 should be understood, then, as referring to the *Diaspora*, i.e., the Jews living outside of Palestine. In 10:14-21 we may picture Paul arguing with the same imaginary opponent who defended the Jews in 3:1-8 (see 2:17–3:20, note 2). This time the objection is that God cannot blame his people for not believing in Jesus as their Messiah since many of them live outside of Palestine and, consequently, have never even heard of Jesus. How can they call on him of whom they have never heard? "Unless your Jesus sends a messenger to preach to them, Paul, how can he find fault?"

Paul's answer is that his kinsmen *have* heard of the righteousness of faith in Christ, no matter where under heaven they may live. Practicing Jews have the Old Testament Scriptures, which proclaim the coming Christ and righteousness by faith so clearly that they have no excuse. Paul's quotation of Psalm 19 is significant here: the *law* of the Lord, the Word of God, reveals God and his way of righteousness with sufficient clarity to bring life to the soul (Ps. 19:7).

Yes, even those Jews who lived far from Palestine and were unfamiliar with the life and teaching of Jesus knew of righteousness by faith based on the coming, death, and resurrection of the Messiah. Yet Israel, having heard the truth, rejected it and persisted in seeking to establish their own righteousness by works of the law (see note 1). Furthermore, as Paul discovered when he preached the gospel to the Gentiles, the Jews resented that the gospel found a hearing among the heathen and thus opposed him at every turn (Acts 13:44-50; 14:1-6; 17:1-5, 10-13; 18:12; 20:3; 21:27-28). Except for a remnant chosen by grace, the Jews refused to enter the kingdom of heaven themselves and hindered others from entering (Matt. 23:37; Luke 11:52).

LESSON 14
Romans 11:1-36

1. Has God rejected Israel? Justify your answer. (11:1-6)

2. In the final analysis, what has kept the mass of Jews from receiving the gospel? (11:7-10)

3. What is God's purpose in hardening most of Israel? (11:11-12)

4. What has resulted from the unbelief of the Jews? (11:12, 30-32)

5. What has resulted from the salvation of the Gentiles? (11:14, 19)

6 What will result at last from the jealousy of Israel? (11: 15-16, 26, 31)

7. Paul warns against an attitude that Gentile Christians might harbor toward the Jews. (11:17-24)

   a. What is that attitude?

   b. Why is it *wrong?*

   c. Why is it *dangerous?*

8. What secret does Paul reveal to his readers? (11:25-32)

9. Why does he reveal this secret? (11:25, 33-36)

STUDY NOTES

1. What Is at Stake: The Faithfulness of God

Most of Israel rejected God's way of righteousness through faith in Christ. Yet Israel's unbelief was entirely within the operation of God's sovereign grace. God chose to have mercy on a few, opening their eyes to the truth and granting them faith in Christ, while he passed by most, hardening them in their sins and leaving them to the futile pursuit of a righteousness based on works of the law. When we contemplate God's sovereign grace and Israel's rejection of Christ at the same time, we may wonder whether or not God has rejected Israel. Has he cast them off forever? Has he chosen a new people, the church, to replace his first people? If so, what does this change in God's purpose imply regarding his faithfulness—and *our* security? And, if God has not rejected Israel, why has he hardened all but a few of them in unbelief?

What is at stake, in Paul's view, is nothing less than the faithfulness of God. Paul entirely vindicates the faithfulness of God as he brings this section of Romans to a close. He shows that God has not rejected Israel, that their unbelief is working toward the salvation of the Gentiles, and that finally "all Israel will be saved" (11:26).

2. The Remnant

One reason for Paul's faith that God has not rejected Israel is the existence of a faithful *remnant*. Although Israel as a whole has rejected Christ and God's way of righteousness through faith in him, a small number of Jews since the coming of Jesus have accepted Jesus as their Messiah and trust in him alone as their righteousness. These faithful Israelites constitute the *remnant*.

The concept of a *remnant* was not Paul's brainchild; it is found throughout the Old Testament. God warned the Israelites in the wilderness that he would reduce them to few in number if they did not obey his voice (Deut. 28:62), and the history of Israel proved God true to his Word. Paul cites the case of Elijah, who believed himself to be the only faithful survivor of King Ahab's cruel persecutions. God informed Elijah that he had reserved for himself a remnant of 7,000 men who had not bowed down to the false god Baal (1 Kings 19:9-10, 13-14, 18). Later, during the reign of King Hezekiah, only a remnant of Jews survived the siege of Jerusalem by the Assyrians (2 Kings 19:4, 30-31). Still later, only a small band of Jews returned to Palestine after they had been captives in Babylon for 70 years (Ezra 9:8). The prophets also had affirmed on various occasions that God would preserve only a remnant of his people (Isa. 1:9; 10:22; 11:11; Jer. 3:14; 5:18; 23:3; 31:7; 44:28; Ezek. 6:8; Joel 2:32; Amos 5:3; Mic. 2:12; Zeph. 2:7; 3:13; Zech. 8:12). In all these instances Israel deserved complete destruction for her sins. Only because of his covenant love did God preserve even a remnant of the people.

Actually, a remnant (Greek: *leimma*, from the verb *leipo*, meaning to *leave* or *leave behind*) is a pitifully small portion, the "leavings" of the people. Is God satisfied with the "leftovers" of Israel? Not at all. The history of Israel and the Word of God show that God claims the whole people. None of the Old Testament events or prophecies cited above supports the idea that God is content to regard a mere remnant of his people as the whole people. The preservation of a remnant was always seen as a promise that someday God would reclaim and restore the entire nation. The remnant is not God's full portion; it is the first fruits of a full harvest, the earnest of his inheritance.

God promised Israel through Moses that he would make them numerous again if only they would repent and return to him (Deut. 30:1-5). God revealed to Elijah that better days were in store for Israel under the prophetic ministry of Elisha and the kingship of Jehu (1 Kings 19:16-17). As for the remnant of Jerusalem in the days of Hezekiah, God promised that it would survive the Assyrian siege and then go forth, be established in the land, and increase (2 Kings 19:30-31). The remnant that returned from exile in Babylon believed that God would bless them if they repented and reformed their lives according to his law (Ezra 10:2-4; Neh. 9–11). Their hope was in accord with the teachings of the prophets, who prophesied more of the restoration of a great number of Israelites than of the tiny remnant (Isa. 26:15; 44:1-5; 45:25; 49:14-21; 54:2-3; 56:8; 60:21-22; Jer. 3:16; 30:19; 33:22; Ezek. 37:26; Mic. 4:6-7; Zech. 8:4-8, 11-13; 10:8-12).

Paul's view of the remnant is in complete agreement with the Old Testament concept. "At the present time" (verse 5) only a remnant cleaves to God, but in God's good time "all Israel will be saved." The existence of a remnant confirms that God will once again stretch forth his hand and save the great majority of Jews.

3. Why Only a Remnant?

It is God's fixed purpose to save all Israel (11:26), yet at the present time he has chosen to save only an elect remnant. God's act of election serves his eternal purpose (9:11), but what is that purpose? Why doesn't God save all Israel now?

In Romans 11 Paul discloses to his readers as much of God's purpose in election as God has chosen to reveal. Briefly, God's purpose is that salvation comes to the Gentiles through the unbelief of the Jews. Then, in God's own time, when the full number of elect Gentiles have come to salvation in Christ, he will remove the hardening of Israel and the Jews will recognize and accept their Messiah. God intended the unbelief of the Jews to advance the salvation of the Gentiles; he intends the faith of the Gentiles to lead to the salvation of the Jews, to the end that "all Israel will be saved."

But that is not all. The salvation of the great mass of Israelites will bring blessing to the world that Paul describes as "life from the dead" (verse 15). Perhaps he is referring to the resurrection. This would imply that Christ will return to judge the world immediately after Israel is converted. Perhaps he is referring figuratively to the blessings of the millennium. Since Paul does not expand on his reference to "life from the dead," we may not use Romans 11 to support any particular theories of eschatology. (Eschatology is the doctrine of the last things, i.e., the return of Christ, the last judgment, the end of the world, and the eternal state of the righteous and the wicked.) Whatever Paul may mean by "life from the dead," he certainly affirms that the Gentiles will be blessed far more by the salvation of Israel than by Israel's fall.

4. Israel and the Church

Paul reaffirms an Old Testament theme when he teaches that the

Gentiles will be blessed through and along with Israel (11:11-12, 15, 17-18). God told Abraham that all nations would be blessed in him (Gen. 18:18). This promise was repeated in the Psalms (45:1-12; 47; 67; 68:28-32; 72:1-11, 17; 86:9; 96:7-13; 98:3-4, 9; 100:1; 138:4-5) and in the prophets, especially Isaiah (see Isa. 11:1-10; 25:6-8; 27:6; 42:1-7; 45:22-23; 51:4-5; 55:3-5; 60:3-4ff.; 66:18-20, 23; also Dan. 7:27; Amos 9:11-12; Mic. 7:16-17; Zeph. 3:9-10, 19-20; Zech. 8:11-13, 22-23; 14:9, 16).

However, the Old Testament did not reveal the manner in which the Gentiles would be blessed in Abraham. The manner of their blessing, which Paul calls a mystery unknown in previous generations (Eph. 3:4-6), is that Gentile believers are made full members of God's people Israel. They are part of the same body, grafted into the same olive tree, as much the children of Abraham as natural-born Jews who share the faith of Abraham (Gal. 3:7-9, 14, 26-29; Eph. 1:9-10; 2:11-19; 3:4-6).

This truth was indeed a mystery before the Holy Spirit revealed it to the apostles and prophets of the apostolic age (Acts 15:7-29; Eph. 3:4-6). The Jews expected that the Gentiles would be separate (and unequal—inferior) recipients of whatever blessings the Old Testament promised them. The law made provision for Gentile converts to the faith of Israel (Num. 9:14; Deut. 23:8), and the Pharisees of Jesus' day carried out an extensive missionary enterprise (see Matt. 23:15). Yet no Jew expected that Gentile converts would ever out-number natural-born Jews. Paul, however, boldly teaches that both a great number of Gentiles will be saved and that they are saved by being grafted into the very same body of which believing Jews are members. In short, Paul teaches that the church and God's true Israel are one and the same body (Gal. 6:16).

Unhappily, this wonderful truth is still a mystery in wide sections of the church today. Worse, it is consciously rejected by many Christians. A common, erroneous view is that the church is a *new*, *second* people of God, distinct and different from his ancient people Israel. According to this theory God has made different promises to Israel and to the church and has ordained them to different destinies: Israel has been promised an earthly kingdom with Jesus ruling in Jerusalem over all the nations of the earth, while the church has been promised a purely spiritual reign with Christ in heaven. Those who hold such views usually maintain that a great many Old Testament prophecies relating to Israel's restoration, prosperity, and worldwide dominion under the Messiah do not find their fulfillment in the salvation of the church and the worldwide spread of the gospel in the present age (the classical, historical interpretation of Protestants and Roman Catholics alike). Instead, adherents of these erroneous teachings believe that many Old Testament prophecies must await fulfillment in a future age since the Jews remain almost completely unreconciled to Christ in the present church age. Such adherents maintain that Israel must be separate and distinct from the church if God's promises to Israel in the Old Testament are to be fulfilled literally.

The classical, historical Protestant (and Roman Catholic) reply is that the *New Testament* clearly identifies the church as God's Israel. Hence, we should read the Old Testament in the light of the New and see the fulfillment of Old Testament prophecies concerning Israel in the past, present, or future life of the church. Admittedly, interpreters differ regarding the precise manner in which these prophecies have been, are being, or shall be fulfilled. (Will there be a millennium? Will Christ come before or after the millennium? Is the millennium now?) However, those who regard Israel and the church as two different peoples have more serious difficulties than simple differences of interpretation. They are compelled time and time again to twist the Scriptures' natural meaning. Most damaging to their position, of course, is the clear teaching of such passages as Romans 11.

Paul's teaching in Romans 11 is in complete agreement with his teaching elsewhere (Gal. 3; Eph. 1–3), with the teaching of the rest of the New Testament (Matt. 8:11; John 10:16; Acts 15:7-18; 1 Pet. 2:9-10), and with the teaching of the Old Testament (see references above). God has only one people, Israel. He intends to bless the world through Israel by grafting a multitude of Gentiles which no man can number (Rev. 7:9) into the stock of Israel. His purpose is that the elect of all nations may be incorporated into Israel through faith in Christ and so may enjoy the blessings promised to Abraham and to his Offspring, Jesus Christ (Gal. 3:29).

5. "All Israel will be saved" (11:26)

Paul explains in 11:1-24 that the present unbelief of Israel is part of God's plan for the salvation of the elect Gentiles. He also implies that God intends to gather fallen Israel to himself once he has accomplished his purpose for the Gentiles (Luke 21:24). As Paul concludes his argument in 11:25-32, he states explicitly what he has implied heretofore: when the full number of Gentiles have come in, "all Israel will be saved" (verse 26).

Most commentators have taken the phrase "all Israel will be saved" to mean that God will remove Israel's blindness and hardness of heart some day and convert the great majority of surviving Jews to Christ (Jer. 31:31-34; Ezek. 36:24-26ff.). Some commentators, however, understand "all Israel" to mean simply the full number of elect Jews and Gentiles, since the church is the Israel of God (Gal. 6:16). According to this view Paul is simply asserting that the hardening of most of Israel is God's means of bringing the elect of all nations to salvation and has nothing to say about the future conversion of the Jews. A careful reading of Romans 9–11, however, shows that Paul has been using the term *Israel* here to mean the Jewish people, whatever wider meaning he may attach to it in other writings. We have seen, moreover, that the preservation of a remnant guarantees the salvation of the mass of the people (note 2). The sanctification of the first fruits makes the whole lump of dough holy (Num. 15:17-21); the sanctification of the root hallows the branches (11:16). We may conclude safely with the majority of commentators that some day the Jews as a people will turn in faith to Jesus as their Messiah.

When will the conversion of the Jews be realized? Romans 11 gives no answer, except that it will happen when the full number of elect Gentiles have been saved (verse 25). The Lord Jesus declared that the gospel must be preached throughout the whole world and then the end will come (Matt. 24:14). Viewing these truths side by side, we can conclude that the conversion of Israel will occur at the end of the age, after the elect Gentiles from every nation have been saved and prior to Christ's return.

Questions remain. Paul states that the conversion of the Jews will lead to even greater blessings for the Gentiles than those flowing from their unbelief (11:12, 15). Does this imply a millennial age after the return of Christ? A millennium *after* the Jews are converted but *before* Christ returns? Or is Paul referring to the blessings of the resurrection and the eternal state? Romans 11 does not furnish us with enough material to answer these questions. Paul's purpose in revealing the mystery of Israel's future conversion is not to give us a view of the future, but, rather, to vindicate God's faithfulness.

6. *The Unsearchable Ways of God*

Human reason would never have surmised that Israel's refusal to acknowledge Jesus as the Christ was part of God's plan to bring the gospel to the Gentiles. Neither does the world believe that God will turn all Israel to Christ some day. God's plan, though, is in agreement with his character. It extends his salvation to all nations even while maintaining his faithfulness to Israel; it is also in complete accord with the promises of Scripture and with Old Testament prophecy. But even Christians, who know the character, promises, and prophecies of God through the Word and the witness of the Spirit, would never have guessed that God purposed both the fall and rising again of Israel for the salvation of the world. His ways are *unsearchable*.

The world will not, indeed, cannot acknowledge that God is actively at work in and through *all* things to accomplish his purpose in the world. Even believers, who gladly confess the workings of sovereign grace in their lives, frequently fail to recognize God's control over the choices and actions of unbelievers. And even when we acknowledge by faith that God is at work in current events, we generally cannot see how those events serve to bring about God's announced ends. His ways are *unsearchable*.

Paul concludes this section of Romans with praise. God has lifted the curtain enough for us to see that even in the most tragic event of history, Israel's rejection of Christ, God was at work to fulfill his plan and purpose. He is faithful to his people Israel. His love does embrace all nations. He is in complete control. Though his ways are unsearchable, He has made them known to us so that we may praise and glorify him for his faithfulness, love, power, and unsearchable wisdom. Praise the Lord!

IV. *CHRISTIAN LIVING*

LESSON 15
Romans 12:1-21

1. What is a *sacrifice?* (Exod. 20:24; Lev. 1:7-9; Deut. 12:27)

2. What does it mean for us to offer our bodies as "living sacrifices"? (12:1; also 6:12-13; 8:1-14)

3. How can we know what is God's "good, pleasing and perfect will" for us? (12:2)

4. What are the characteristics of a renewed, transformed mind? (12:3)

5. What relationship do Christians have to one another? To what does Paul compare our relationship? (12:4-5)

6. Why does God give us gifts? (12:6-8)

7. What are we to do with the gifts God has given us? (12:6-8)

8. How can you find out what your own gifts are? (12:3)

9. What motivates us to use the gifts we have received? (12:1-5)

10. What hinders us from using these gifts? (12:3b, 6b)

11. What attitudes are we to cultivate toward fellow Christians? (12:9-13, 16; also Gal. 5:19-26, especially verses 22-26)

12. What attitudes are we to cultivate toward our neighbors, whether they are fellow Christians or not? (12:14-21)

13. Can we expect to get along well with our neighbors and our fellow Christians when we live according to Paul's admonitions? (12:14-21)

STUDY NOTES

1. Living for God

Having proclaimed all that God has done, is doing, and will do for us in chapters 1–11, Paul now turns to what *we* should do and how *we* should live in chapters 12–16. As we study these chapters, we should bear in mind that they not only *follow* chapters 1–11, they also *follow from* those earlier chapters.

What God has done for us is the foundation of what we should do for God. "Therefore" (12:1), because of everything related in chapters 1–11, what follows is the *logical service* we owe God. The Greek phrase rendered "spiritual worship" in the NIV is *logiken latreian*, better translated *logical, reasonable, or rational service*. Our *logiken latreian* is the kind of life that follows from the fact that we have received the mercy of God. Because we are dead to sin and alive to God (6:11-13), because we are dead to the law (7:4-6), because we are no longer in the flesh and controlled by the sinful nature (8:9-11), and because God is faithful and will keep us to the end (8:28-39)—for all these reasons we can and must live a new life for God, confident that losing our life for his sake is actually saving it (Mark 8:35; also 2 Cor. 5:15-17)

2. Members of One Body

The radical reorientation of our thinking for which Paul calls in 12:2 has two aspects. The first is the realization that living for God is the service we logically owe him as a result of our salvation (note 1). The second is the consciousness that we do not exist and live as isolated, individual believers. We are members of one another; we all belong to a single spiritual body whose Head is Christ (12:5; see also 1 Cor. 12:12, 27; Eph. 4:4, 15-16). The service we owe God is not merely a matter of our personal relationship with him; it is also a matter of our relationship with other believers. The truth that we are members of the same body and of one another was implicit in chapter 11, where Paul likens us to the branches of a single olive tree. Now Paul addresses this doctrine explicitly and expounds its implications for Christian living.

To view ourselves and other believers as members of one another is the function of a transformed mind. The worldly mind, the old nature, is egocentric and individualistic—at least in much of Western society. Our society promotes *individual* rights, *personal* achievement, *personal* development, *self*-expression, *self*-actualization, and rugged *individualism*. Even the group values we prize, such as cooperation and majority rule, are directed toward maximizing the freedom and well-being of the individual. In our society groups as such have no rights apart from the individuals who make them up. But the minds of those in traditional or collectivist societies are equally conformed to the world. People may be less individualistic in such societies, but their loyalty is to the family, clan, state, or some other social unit based on natural or artificial principles and not on spiritual unity in Christ.

Christians, on the other hand, are called to view themselves as members of a spiritual body. All who have been cleansed by the blood of Christ are citizens of God's commonwealth, members of his people Israel (Eph. 2:19; see also Rom. 11:1-36, note 4). We may have few or no natural bonds or common interests uniting us. Paul's original readers, for instance, represented the most diverse natural backgrounds—some slaves and others masters, some foreigners and others native Romans, some Jews and others Gentiles (see Rom. 1:1-17, note 3). Yet they all had one thing in common: Christ and the spiritual blessings found in him (Eph. 1:3-10, 22-23).

Sadly, Protestants have largely lost sight of the truth that all God's people constitute a single spiritual body whose members are members of each other. We show our lack of consciousness of the one body in many ways: by our willingness to split and divide and remain separated from one another for reasons far removed from the essentials of the faith; by the fact that our churches rarely cross social, economic, or racial lines, and by our failure to use the gifts God has given us for the benefit of our brothers and sisters (see note 3) or even to care very much about their welfare. Finally, we show our lack of consciousness of the one body of Christ by failing to seek the fruit of our brothers' gifts. If we were fully aware of being members of one another, then we would encourage one another to use the gifts God has given us; we would know that we cannot progress very far in our own sanctification without each other's help, and we would make every effort to maintain and strengthen peace, unity of mind, and cooperation in the body of Christ.

Paul expounds the truth of the unity of God's people more fully in other writings (1 Cor. 3:1-23; 12:4-31; Eph. 2:11-22; 4:1-16). This truth underlies the rest of Romans: chapters 12, 14, 15, and 16 assume as understood that believers have a special relationship to each other as members of one body whose well-being depends on the harmony existing between the members.

3. Spiritual Gifts

Paul means to stress two truths when he likens us to the limbs and organs of a body. The first, discussed in note 2, is that we are members of one another. We are so related to each other that we cannot live for God without taking notice of our brothers and sisters in Christ.

The second truth conveyed by the metaphor of the body with its limbs and organs is that we have been given different functions in the church, different ways of serving Christ. As the parts of a body are different, yet the body remains one and the parts all act together to promote the good of the whole body, so we have different functions to carry out, yet we all work together toward a common end.

Our abilities to carry out these different functions are gifts from God's indwelling Spirit, not natural abilities that unbelievers might also possess. When we look at other passages dealing with God's gifts, in particular 1 Corinthians 12:4-31 (see also Eph. 4:7-13 and 1 Pet. 4:10-11), we see that these gifts are all manifestations of the Holy Spirit. Since only believers are indwelt by the Holy Spirit (Rom. 8:9, 14), these gifts are possessed only by believers.

When we compare Romans 12 with 1 Corinthians 12:8-10, Ephesians 4:11, and 1 Peter 4:10-11, we see that the list of spiritual gifts given here is not exhaustive or complete. Indeed, there is no reason to believe that these passages taken together list all the spiritual gifts that God in his grace gives to the church. On the other hand, comparing these passages side by side makes it clear that certain gifts are more important for the church than others. Apostles, prophets, and teachers are mentioned more frequently and are given a more prominent place than, for instance, those having the gift of tongues.

The question of whether all the gifts listed in the New Testament are still present in the church is not answered in these passages, but we can safely conclude on other grounds that apostleship, prophecy, and the miraculous gifts are no longer given to the church. By their very nature, such gifts were foundational for the church and its mission. The foundation was laid, and now these gifts have ceased. (It would be too much of a digression to enter into proof of this assertion. Those interested should read Calvin's *Institutes*, book IV, chapter 3, sections 1-8.)

The particular gifts enumerated in 12:6-8 are:

a. *Prophecy:* delivering or speaking the truth of God as given to the prophet by direct revelation.

b. *Service* (Greek: *diakonia):* meeting the material needs of the hungry, homeless, sick, afflicted, and destitute. Our word *deacon* comes from the Greek *diakonos,* a related word. This gift may refer specifically to ordained deacons, although not necessarily since the words *diakonia* and *diakonos* are so general in meaning.

c. *Teaching:* speaking and applying the truth of God as received from the apostles and prophets (not as received by direct revelation), i.e., expounding the Word of God.

d. *Encouraging:* speaking to the heart to encourage and strengthen and move to action; sometimes rendered *exhortation.*

e. *Contributing:* giving to the material needs of the poor.

f. *Leadership:* governing or ruling the church of God. This gift is exercised by the elders (Greek: *presbuteroi)* and bishops (Greek: *episkopoi)*—terms used interchangeably in the New Testament. The gift was also exercised by the apostles.

g. *Showing mercy:* giving direct help to those in need. This service is more personal than contributing; it need not involve material aid.

The gifts of service, teaching, encouraging, contributing, leadership, and showing mercy are not merely the natural abilities denoted by the same words. An unbeliever might be a good teacher in the secular world, but he would not be a good teacher in the church. Intellectual understanding and good technique are not enough! Similarly, an unbelieving executive may possess excellent leadership skills for business, politics, or civic affairs, but he does not qualify for church service. Leadership in the church requires more than interpersonal skills, decision-making ability, and the capacity to plan, organize, and delegate authority.

On the other hand, a believer gifted by God with teaching ability may well be an excellent teacher in the public schools as well, and a Christian with leadership ability may well exercise his or her gift successfully in the business world, too. In fact—and here is a danger

of which Paul was well aware—a believer may use his or her gift in
the world but fail to use it for the benefit of the church family. Too
many believers use their God-given talents only for themselves
rather than for the good of the body as God intended. Hence, Paul
stresses (verses 6-8) that we are to *use* our gifts for each other's
benefit and for the entire church.

Another danger exists with regard to the use of spiritual gifts.
Many Christians do not use their gifts at all, either for the church or
for their personal benefit. Why not? Some Christians do not believe
they have any spiritual gifts. Yet Paul suggests here (and declares
explicitly in 1 Corinthians 12:7) that *every* Christian has some manifestation of the Spirit for the common good, and some even have
more than one gift. If you do not know what your gift is, you need to
evaluate yourself objectively (12:3) to determine what it may be,
perhaps asking other believers for their insights.

A third danger exists with respect to spiritual gifts. It is all too easy
to disdain the gifts of other Christians. We need constantly to
remind ourselves that God has so ordained that *none* of us has all the
spiritual resources he or she needs. All of us need every one of our
brothers and sisters and their gifts just as they need us and our gifts
(1 Cor. 12:21-26). The body can grow into what God intends it to be
only when each part functions properly (Eph. 4:16).

4. Christian Behavior

After exhorting us to use our spiritual gifts for each other's benefit, Paul admonishes us in 12:9-21 to practice certain kinds of behavior toward each other and the world. These exhortations are for
all believers; no one needs a special gift to make them part of his or
her life. Verses 9-13 are directed mostly toward our relationships
with other Christians; verses 14-21 have in view our relationships
with the world. The attitudes and practices commended here are
listed in the answers to study questions 11 and 12 (12:1-21 in Appendix B) and will not be reiterated here. Nevertheless two points
merit comment.

First, although we are all urged to contribute to the needs of our
fellow Christians, only some have the special spiritual gift of contributing (cf. verse 8ba with 13a). This suggests that the spiritual gift
of contributing involves steady, continual giving. Does that fact
imply that this particular gift is primarily given to the wealthy—

those with the means to give much as well as the ability to identify the truly needy and to give to them without fuss or fanfare, saving the dignity of the recipient? Or is the spiritual gift of contributing given to those in the church entrusted with church funds for this purpose, i.e., the deacons? The first alternative is more probable, for those with the gift of contributing are urged to do so liberally, implying that they give away their own money. The emphasis of verse 13a, however, must be borne in mind by all Christians. Whether wealthy or not, all of us are commanded to contribute to those in need as we are able.

Second, verse 21 is a summary of verses 14-20: we are to overcome evil by our lives. By this we show that we are living sacrifices wholly given to God. The way we live in the midst of opposition and persecution is a critical test of just how dead to the world we are in practical terms. When attacked, do we revert to the world's way of defending self? If so, we are not living according to the truth that we are dead to sin and alive to God in Christ Jesus.

5. "You will heap burning coals on his head" (12:20)

Verse 20b seems jarringly out of place. Paul has been writing of the need to bless our persecutors, but here he quotes an Old Testament passage (Prov. 25:21-22) that seems to express a contrary wish. Does Paul mean that we can increase our enemies' eternal torment by doing them good when they do us ill (Ps. 140:10)? Everything else in the passage suggests another intention, but what else can verse 20b mean?

One alternative interpretation is that "burning coals" on the head refers figuratively to a burning conscience. Paul's point, then, would be that our good behavior will make our enemies burn with shame at the thought of their evil behavior toward us (1 Pet. 3:16).

While this interpretation may be part of Paul's meaning, the expression almost certainly means more. In harmony with the entirety of 12:14-21, we can assume that Paul is referring in some way to the blessing that our good behavior will bring to our enemies (Matt. 5:11-16, especially verse 16). Simple remorse is not in itself a blessing. Our enemies need salvation; they need to be cleansed from sin. The sin-cleansing sacrifice of Christ is represented in the Old Testament by the sacrifices slain and burned on the altar (Lev. 1–6, especially chapter 4; see also Isa. 6:5-7; Heb. 9:13-14). All things considered, Paul seems to mean that God will move some who see us return good for evil beyond remorse and shame to repentance and the faith that appropriates the sacrifice of Christ for one's self. Figuratively speaking, coals from the altar of sacrifice will be heaped upon them, cleansing them from their sins. In this way evil is *overcome* by good (12:21).

LESSON 16
Romans 13:1-14

1. How are we to *regard* or *view* the governing authorities? (13:1-2, 4)

2. How are we to *behave* toward the governing authorities? (13:1-7)

3. What is the proper, God-ordained role of government? (13:3-6)

4. What kind of debts are we permitted to incur? (13:8ff.)

5. What is the role of the law for the Christian? (13:8-10)

6. What reason does Paul give here for encouraging his readers to live God's way rather than the world's way? (13:11-14)

7. *How* can we live God's way? (13:14)

STUDY NOTES

1. The Legitimacy of the Governing Authorities

Paul lived in an era when Roman emperors came to power by violent means. Augustus, who reigned when Jesus was born; Tiberius, who reigned when he was crucified; Caligula; Claudius, who probably was ruling when Paul wrote Romans, and Nero, who ruled when Paul, according to tradition, was executed in Rome— none of these men came to the throne by natural succession or uncoerced election by the Roman senate. They all assumed the imperial power by force and violence. Their subsequent reigns were marked by deceit, debauchery, violence, and murder at the highest political levels. The history of Paul's own people had also been characterized by political intrigue and violence; many of the kings of Israel and Judah had come to power and maintained their rule by violence and oppression (see 1 and 2 Kings for numerous instances).

In light of the brutal histories of Rome and Israel, how could Paul possibly say that the governing authorities were established and instituted by God? And what are we to say in our own century in light of the regimes of Hitler and the Soviets? Indeed, most modern nations are presently under governments that were originally established by military conquest, coup d'etat, or revolution—including our own! Are all these governments established by God? Are they all legitimate?

Paul knew that God is sovereign over all; he is King of kings and Lord of lords. No one comes to power except by the will and working of God. God is not the author of the ungodly means men use to attain power—but that they come to power is ordained by him. Hence, the Christian has no right to reject the authority of a given government merely because of the means used to come to power. The fact that a government is in power is evidence that God established it.

2. The Mandate of the Governing Authorities

God established the ruling authorities to carry out his purpose. He has charged and obligated them to execute his sentence of wrath on those who do evil and has authorized them to use force for that purpose. They have the right to require our taxes, submission, and respect for the fulfullment of that end. Governments are ordained for our good (verse 4).

Whether they recognize his sovereignty or not, the ruling authorities are responsible to God for carrying out the duties he has laid on them. When governments do not strive to prevent and punish wickedness or do not exercise their powers for our good, they sin against God, and they will suffer judgment for their delinquency.

It is easy to find fault with government. We daily observe its failure to prevent and punish evil. When government does not take the necessary steps to prevent and punish physical violence, such as assault, rape, murder, abortion, theft, and extortion, it sins against God. When it does not make adequate provision for defense in the face of military threat, it also sins against God. When government does not protect the vulnerable against the economic predation of loan sharking, fraud, price-fixing, and "sharp" business practices, it sins against God. And when it does not stem vice—prostitution, pornography, gambling, drugs—it sins against God.

While government sins when it does too little, can it sin by doing too much? God established governments for our good (verse 4). Some Christians maintain that government is to do us good *only* in preventing and punishing wickedness. Others affirm that government also has a mandate to undertake projects and activities that promote the general welfare, even though those activities are not confined to preventing and punishing evil. The Bible gives us very little basis for deciding which position is correct. Joseph advised Pharaoh to collect, store, and distribute food to the Egyptian people during the seven years of famine (Gen. 41:33-36). Solomon built store cities in various locations in Judah, possibly to meet the people's need in a similar circumstance (1 Kings 9:19). Public water supplies existed in Jerusalem in the days of the kings of Judah (Kings 18:17), and Paul himself traveled on publicly maintained Roman roads (Acts 28:13-16). These references are much too inconclusive to direct us to any firm convictions regarding the proper role of government in fostering public welfare.

And the point is moot: governments undertake many diverse activities, and society could not get along without some of them. Governments build bridges, operate schools, carry the mail, sponsor the arts, fight fires, fund and administer entitlement programs such as welfare and social security, maintain public health programs, purchase and maintain public parks and even parking lots. The list of activities carried out in the name of the public good is practically endless. And we are taxed for such activities. Probably no one believes that government ought to be involved in *every* activity for which we pay taxes. What then is the Christian, in good conscience, to do?

3. Submission to the Governing Authorities: Always?

What is the Christian to do when government is not carrying out its divine mandate? What if it fails to protect its citizens from harm or does not punish wickedness or goes beyond the bounds God has set for its activities? What if it engages in unjust, violent, evil behavior?

Paul's teaching seems quite clear. We are to pay our taxes and whatever else we owe without resisting or rebelling against the government. *Our* responsibility is to render to the government what it has the right to demand (Matt. 22:15-21); *government's* responsibility is to use its power and resources to carry out its divine mandate. When the governing authorities do not obey God by either acting or failing to act, it is their sin and not ours. When government exceeds its bounds or fails to execute judgment on those who do evil, it does not absolve us of our duty to give to government what it has a right to demand.

Is civil disobedience *never* justified? Are there no circumstances under which we *must* refuse to submit to government for conscience' sake? Indeed, are there not governments so perverted that rebellion and revolution are called for?

Paul does not indicate any such circumstances in the Book of Romans. However, we know that we ought always to obey God rather than men (Acts 4:18-20). When the choice is between obeying

the Lord of all and obeying a human authority, we must obey God at
all costs. If and when we are compelled by government to participate directly and personally in evil, we must refuse. If we have the
opportunity to change the policy of the government—and we have
that opportunity in a democracy—then we should do what we can.
The Bible, though, gives no comfort to those (whether on the right
or on the left) who would actively resist unjust governments, as long
as the people are not compelled to participate personally in sin or
prohibited from doing right. None of us is called by God, as
was Jeroboam (1 Kings 11:26-38) or Jehu (2 Kings 9:1-37), to over-
throw a wicked government. Let him who so claims point to the
prophet who anointed him! God always overthrows the wicked in
his own time, but not by us.

4. Should the State Defend the Faith?

The Christian message had made little impact on the Roman
world at the time Paul wrote Romans. Not until 250 years later, after
continued growth and intermittent persecution, was the church
taken under the official protection of the Roman state by Emperor
Constantine. He made Christianity the official faith of the empire
and undertook to sponsor, protect, and defend the church. For the
next 1500 years or so, the Roman Empire, its successor states, and
the nations of the New World settled by the European powers
continued to view themselves as sponsors of the church and defenders of the faith. Only in the last 200 years or so have nations with
a Christian heritage disestablished the church and given up the
defense of the faith.

Some Christians today wish that the state were still disposed to
protect and defend the faith of Christ. Although our own government's official stance towards the Christian faith and Christian
churches is one of strict neutrality, the state is all too often hostile in
its actions towards the cause of Christ. What should our position be
regarding the role of the state as the protector and supporter of the
church and the gospel? It may not be realistic to expect that we can
turn our government around and make it avowedly Christian, but
the question is not an idle one. Believers do get elected and appointed to decision-making positions in government. Should Christian officeholders strive to implement specifically biblical principles
as public policy? Ought they to use their public powers to protect,

encourage, and support the church?

Other democratic nations of the West have not separated church and state as completely as has the United States. In some countries Christian schools receive financial support from the government. In others Christian moral principles are part of the law of the land—principles not written into law because they happen to represent the current ethical consensus of the nation, but because they represent the teaching of the Christian church. On the negative side, we can think of countries where the government supports an established church, supposedly Christian, which actually obscures and opposes the pure gospel of Christ. Nevertheless, we must ask: Should the state *in principle* support the church and promote the Christian faith?

The Reformers affirmed that the state, duty-bound by its mandate to do us good (13:4), must support actively true biblical religion. They maintained this position in spite of the fact that they encountered firsthand the opposition of states defending a corrupt faith and opposing the gospel in the very name of Christ. The Reformers and their spiritual descendants for several generations were harassed, persecuted, and martyred for the true faith of Christ. Yet, they affirmed the principle that the state, as God's servant for our good in this world, must support the church and the practice of biblical religion. Such was the position of Calvin, the English Puritans, and the early Scottish Presbyterians—and they implemented it wherever they could attain political power. At the time of our Revolution, American evangelicals did not conceive of the state's duty in terms of supporting a single state church. Nevertheless, they affirmed that the government ought to support Christian moral principles and give aid to the churches without preferring one Christian denomination above another.

We must settle for less today, for practical reasons if for no others. The burden of proof, however, falls on those who would say that Christians in public office ought not, as a matter of principle, to exercise their powers to help us practice our faith more freely and to make the law of God the underlying basis for the law of the land. At the very least, there is no incompatibility between the Scriptures and the position that the state ought to facilitate and aid the practice of our religion. Any argument to the contrary must be founded on practical considerations—e.g., the fact that our society is pluralistic and hostile to the absolute moral standards of the law of God.

5. Debt and the Believer

The NIV reading in 13:8 begins, "Let no debt remain outstanding. . . ." A more literal rendering of the Greek phrase is, "owe
nothing to anyone." Some Christians take Paul's words in the
strongest sense possible, i.e., as a command not to go into debt at
all. But most of us are in debt. Our houses are mortgaged; we have
monthly car payments; we use bank cards and credit cards daily.
Farmers and small businessmen cannot operate without credit.
Even most churches borrow money when they set out to build. If the
strongest interpretation of 13:8 is the proper one, then most believers in America are living in financial sin.

The translators of the NIV apparently did not interpret verse 8 in
the strongest sense possible. Their translation suggests that the
meaning of the Greek is that we should never fall behind in our
payments. When we borrow money, we should have a payment
schedule and adhere to it faithfully.

The Bible says very little about debt, and we cannot decide which
of these two interpretations is correct. In any case, both are radical
views, requiring us to break with this world's pattern and to let our
minds be transformed (12:2). The stronger interpretation is patently
radical in the eyes of American society (although we would secretly
envy anyone who we believed to be entirely debt free). The interpretation suggested by the NIV rendering also requires breaking with
the world; a corollary to this interpretation is that we must exercise
enough restraint and self-control in buying that we avoid getting
into debt over our heads.

Only by the power of God can we find the self-control to resist the
siren call to consume until we have consumed ourselves. We are
submerged in a sea of advertising urging us to buy whatever we
want *now*—and to want what we did not want before. Lack of
money is no problem. Easy credit! Nothing down! Buy now, pay
later! Clever minds in the advertising media are bending their best
efforts toward moving us to desire and spend no matter what the
cost. We are incapable in our own strength of controlling the lusts of
the old nature in this area, just as we cannot control our lusts in
eating, drinking, sex, and anger by ourselves. Self-control is a fruit
of the Holy Spirit (Gal. 5:23; 2 Tim. 1:7). Christians who cannot
control their buying and borrowing must come to realize that such
excess is a sin and that they must clothe themselves with Jesus

Christ (verse 14). This means that they must live by the power of the Holy Spirit as they seek to bring this aspect of their lives under the lordship of Christ. (See also 8:1-17, note 3.)

6. The Law of Love

We are obligated to love one another (verse 8), for in so doing we fulfill the commandments. The commandments are specific applications of the law of love. Jesus made it clear that the law of love goes beyond minimum, external compliance with the letter of the law (Matt. 5:17-48; 22:34-40). Paul is stating no more than that here—and no less. In consideration of the fuzzy talk so common today about love *superseding* the commandments, we must maintain that love *fulfills* them in spirit as well as in letter.

Paul wrote in 8:2 that we now serve in the law of the Spirit. The law of the Spirit is the same as the law of love—the fulfillment of the commandments of God from the heart, by the power of the Spirit (see 8:1-17, note 2).

7. "Our salvation is nearer now than when we first believed" (13:11)

In 13:11 Paul refers to our salvation as a *future* hope. In 8:24 he describes it as a *past* event. In 1 Corinthians 1:18 salvation is described as a *present* reality. The noun *salvation* (Greek: *soteria*) and the verb *save* (Greek: *sozo*) have past, present, and future aspects; they also denote both objective and subjective realities.

a. *Salvation* often refers to the objective work of Christ for his people (Luke 1:69; 2:30; 3:6; Eph. 1:13). Used in this sense, it denotes what Christ did for us rather than our experience of the benefits of his work. It has reference to the work done outside of us as the objective basis for the work done within us and to us when we believe.

b. *Salvation* and *saved* frequently describe our personal justification and regeneration (Luke 19:19; Rom. 1:16). In this sense *salvation* is a past event in the life of the believer, a one-time occurrence initiating the good standing with God (5:1) and new life (6:11) that we continue to enjoy as believers in Christ.

c. In at least one passage (Phil. 2:12), *salvation* refers to the con-

tinuous process of sanctification and deliverance from the power of
sin in the believer's life.

d. In the present passage and others (Phil. 1:28; 1 Thess. 5:9;
Heb.9:28; Rev. 7:10; 12:10; 19:1), *salvation* is a future, eschatological
reality. The word *eschatological* comes from the Greek *eschatos*, meaning *last*, and refers to the events of the last days when the Lord Jesus
returns from heaven. In this future sense "our salvation is nearer
now than when we first believed" (verse 11). It is reassuring that our
complete salvation—past, present, eternal—was secured by Christ
our Savior.

LESSON 17
Romans 14:1-23

STUDY QUESTIONS
1. What does *weak in faith* mean? (14:1-2, 14, 23)

2. What matters were disputed in the church at Rome? (14: 2, 5, 14-17)

3. In general, how are we to behave toward those weak in faith? (14:1, 3, 10, 13-15, 19-21)

4. What is Paul's admonition to the restrictive Christian?

5. What is Paul's command to all Christians, restrictive and permissive? (14:1, 4-12, 13, 18, 19)

6. Why is it wrong to judge a brother's convictions about the kinds of issues under consideration here? (14:8-13a)

7. What constraints limit a Christian's liberty of conduct? (see also 13:8-14)

8. What is wrong with continuing in certain behavior that I know is acceptable to God, even good in itself, when a less mature, weaker brother considers it to be sinful? (14:19-21)

9. Can you think of contemporary issues in the church to which this chapter is especially applicable?

STUDY NOTES

1. Disagreement and Christian Love

Born-again Christians often disagree with each other on matters of faith and life—not on the essentials of the faith, of course, but on issues that all acknowledge to be secondary. As one body in Christ, we ought to treat one another with love and respect even when we disagree (12:3-13; 13:8-10). Sadly, our disputes sometimes strain unity and lead to loveless acts. Doctrinal squabbles over secondary matters frequently produce bad feelings. At times we condemn some believers and look down on others as immature and lacking spiritual perception for their differing views and practices. We staunchly defend our own beliefs on secondary issues as "matters of principle," heedless of the effects of our behavior on the spiritual well-being of our brothers and sisters in Christ.

Possibly the church in Rome experienced such internal disputes; at least, Paul was concerned it might. The apostle takes up the question of disagreements over secondary matters in this chapter. His purpose is not to render a definitive ruling on each dispute in the early church (although he does indicate clearly how things stand on the issue of unclean foods). Rather, his purpose is to call his readers to live so as to strengthen each other and the church. It is far more important to work for the peace, unity, and edification of God's people than to maintain our own opinions and rights against all comers no matter what the cost. As we study chapter 14, let us determine both to learn and to put into practice the lesson Paul teaches here.

2. *Disputable Matters*

We need to be able to differentiate between the essential truths of the faith, secondary truths, and matters of indifference. Essential truths of the faith are not disputable, though they may be disputed; indeed, we *must* contend for them whenever they are challenged or denied. Secondary truths must never be denied, but we need not always actively contend for them. Matters of indifference ought not to be disputed unless someone makes such a matter one of obedience or belief for all or, worse, an essential of the faith; we must then refute such a false teaching.

Essentials of the faith are truths that one must believe to be saved or, at least, that a saved person may not deny (understandably, a young Christian may be ignorant of some essential doctrines). The doctrines of the Trinity, the incarnation, the vicarious atonement and resurrection of Christ are some essential truths. We must stand firm for the essentials of the faith even though division and controversy result. The Lord's people will recognize and cling to the truth when disputed and challenged (John 10:1-5, 14-16; 16:13-15; 1 Cor. 11:18-19; 1 John 2:18-19).

Secondary truths are matters revealed in Scripture or deduced with certainty from Scripture that are not essentials of the gospel faith. The truth of infant baptism is an example of a secondary truth; it can be deduced with certainty from Scripture (see 4:13-25, note 2), but belief in infant baptism is not essential for salvation. Other examples of secondary truths are the imputation of Adam's sin (see 5:1-21, note 4) and the identity of Israel and the church (see 11:1-36, note 4).

All secondary truths are not of equal importance and do not have equal implications for our obedience. We must contend for a secondary truth (remembering all the while that it is secondary) whenever personal obedience demands it. For example, since baptizing our children is a matter of obedience to God, we dare not forego infant baptism in the interest of peace and unity; but, since it is not an essential of the faith, we may not require believers to baptize their children as a condition of church membership. Other secondary truths do not entail obedience to God, and we need not always contend publicly for such truths. For example, in spite of what some believers in Rome thought, Christians may eat meat (note 3). Yet Scripture does not require us to eat meat. The truth that all foods are clean (Mark 7:19) does not entail obedience or disobedience. We ought to believe this principle, for it is scriptural, but we do not need to contend openly for it unless someone begins to teach that obedience to God requires all Christians to refrain from meat.

Matters of indifference (Greek: *adiophora*, meaning *not to be preferred*, i.e., on which the position taken does not matter) are practices about which, for lack of biblical directives clear enough to establish a general rule, God's Word allows freedom of individual conscience. May Christians use tobacco? May they celebrate Christmas? How about Halloween? Is it all right to drink alcoholic beverages in moderation? Such questions are considered *adiaphora* by some believers; others believe they can deduce from Scripture a definite affirmative or negative answer to each of these questions. It is precisely the kind of issue that is a matter of indifference to one and a matter of principle to another that gives rise to the kind of dispute Paul deals with in chapter 14.

3. Why Vegetarianism?

One issue disputed in the church at Rome was the eating of meat. Some believed they could eat all foods, including meat, while others ate "only vegetables" as a matter of principle.

Who were these vegetarian Christians in the church at Rome? They cannot have been Jewish converts who still felt obligated to keep the Jewish dietary laws, for the law of Moses did not forbid the eating of meat in general, only the eating of certain kinds of meat. Paul clearly states that those who would not eat meat are among the weak in faith, since there is nothing inherently wrong in eating meat (verses 2, 14, 20). Why did some first-century believers think that eating meat was sinful?

A likely reason for their scruples is suggested by a comparison of Romans 14 with 1 Corinthians 8:1-13 and 10:23-33. Much of the meat sold in the cities of the Roman Empire, such as Corinth, came from pagan temples, where a worshiper would bring an animal to be sacrificed. Part of the animal's flesh would be offered to the god on the altar, and part would be consumed by the worshipers in a ritual meal on the temple grounds. The remainder of the meat would be sold in the public market to provide income for the temple. Some recent converts in Corinth had such a strong sense of the religious significance of eating temple meat that any eating of meat amounted to participation in a pagan religious rite. Since they could not be sure whether meat bought in the public market had not been consecrated to an idol, the safe thing for them was to abstain from all meat. It is not certain whether or not the vegetarians in the church at Rome acted from the same motives as those in the Corinthian church, but the source of meat must have been the same in both cities. Paul's admonition to the stronger brother is essentially the same in both cases (cf. Rom. 14:15-16, 20-23 with 1 Cor. 8:9-13; 10:23-33).

Among twentieth-century Christians only Seventh-Day Adventists are vegetarians as a group (though not all of them practice it). They base their abstinence from meat on the teaching of Ellen G. White, one of their founders, whom they consider to have been a prophetess. Are we to refrain from disputing with them on the issue of eating meat when the question arises? No. We should argue from Scripture against Adventist vegetarianism when the issue is raised, for their belief rests on the false and dangerous doctrine that Mrs. White was inspired by God. The real issue here is not vegetarianism, but whether or not God has revealed himself through one of their founders. Our Lord was not silent when the traditions of men were opposed to the Word of God (Mark 7:1-8), and we dare not remain silent either when that is the real issue. But let all our debates with Seventh-Day Adventists be carried out in patience, gentleness, and love (2 Tim. 2:23-26); they are members of a genuine Christian church in spite of this and other errors.

4. Is the Weekly Sabbath for the Weak?

Paul indicates in 14:5-6 that a disagreement arose in the church at Rome over the keeping of holy days. Some believed one day to be more sacred than the rest while others treated all days alike. What kinds of days were under consideration? Were they the Jewish feasts? Was the weekly Sabbath a matter of controversy? We cannot be absolutely certain what kinds of days were disputed in Rome; the reference in verses 5 and 6 is too brief. But disputes over observing special days occurred in other churches to which Paul wrote, namely those in Galatia and Colossae. Those disputes suggest some kinds of disagreements that may have troubled the church at Rome.

The Galatian churches seem to have begun observing all the Jewish holy days after Paul left them (Gal. 4:9-11). Believers in Colossae were under pressure to do the same (Col. 2:16-17). Paul tells both the Galatians and the Colossians that they are not obligated to keep the Jewish holy days; indeed, he suggests strongly that they ought not to keep them. It is possible, even likely, that the controversy in Rome was over the observance of the Jewish holy days also.

However, while he is definitely against celebrating the Jewish holy days in Galatia and Colossae, Paul is neutral with regard to the disagreement in Rome. If the issue in Rome was the same as in Galatia and Colossae, then why was his response to the Romans different?

Perhaps the difference was that the Romans who celebrated the Jewish holy days did not seek to impose them as an obligation on the whole church. The observance of the Jewish holy days may have been a matter of indifference in Rome, neither commanded nor forbidden, and all would have known it. In Galatia and Colossae, however, some had elevated a matter of indifference to a matter of obedience for all Christians. In such a case Paul had to contend for the truth of the gospel; Christ fulfilled the law, and the ceremonies that were but shadows of Christ have been rendered obsolete and unnecessary (Col. 2:17; also Heb. 10:1). We also must contend openly for the truth that matters of indifference are not issues of obedience whenever they are elevated to the status of obligations (note 2).

Does the weekly Sabbath fall in the same category as the Jewish holy days? Is it a matter of indifference? These are questions of importance for us today. Should we oppose those who elevate the Sabbath to a matter of obedience for all Christians? Far from it! The contrary is the case. We must recognize and prove to doubters that the Sabbath commandment has abiding validity.

When taken as a whole, the Scriptures clearly teach that the Sabbath is not in the same category as the yearly and monthly Jewish holy days. The Sabbath commandment is contained in the Decalogue, the Ten Commandments (Exod. 19:8-11; Deut. 5:12-15). The Decalogue expresses the abiding moral law of love for God and man (13:8-10; also Matt. 22:34-40). The Sabbath, antedating the giving of the law to Israel on Sinai, is a creation ordinance for the entire human race (Gen. 2:2-3). Jesus declared that the Sabbath was made for *man*—not for Israel alone but for generic man (Mark 2:27). Mark records that Jesus abolished the dietary restrictions that had been given to Israel only (7:14-19), but he also records that Jesus affirmed the universal Sabbath. Finally, prophecies of the future reign of Christ refer to the perpetuity of the Sabbath (Isa. 66:22-23; Ezek. 44:24). True, such prophecies must be read for their spiritual meaning. Nevertheless, they express the reality of an abiding Sabbath for God's people. On the basis of such Scriptures, we conclude that the weekly Sabbath cannot be in view in Romans 14.

Does not Paul refer specifically to the Sabbath day in Colossians 2:16? Indeed he does, and he has the weekly Sabbath in view in Colossians. Some defenders of the weekly Sabbath have sought to interpret *Sabbath* in Colossians 2:16 as a generic term for special, nonweekly sabbaths (e.g., the sabbath of Lev. 16:31). But it is clear from Colossians 2:16 that Paul has in view the *yearly* religious festivals, the *monthly* New Moon celebrations, and the *weekly* Sabbath days. The issue in Colossae was not whether a weekly Sabbath day should be kept but whether *Jewish* feasts should be obligatory. Must the church in Colossae keep the weekly Jewish Sabbath on Saturday or keep the weekly Lord's day on Sunday, the day of Christ's resurrection? Paul tells the Colossians that they should let no one take them to task for not celebrating the Jewish holy days, including the Saturday Sabbath, but he is not absolving them of the command to keep a weekly day holy to the Lord.

In the light of all that the Bible says about the abiding nature of the weekly Sabbath *and* in consideration of what it says about the abolition of any obligation to keep the cermonial law, the real issue seems to be whether the Christian Sabbath must be kept on Saturday, the old Sabbath day, or on Sunday, the day of the Lord's resurrection. On this issue Paul has nothing to say in the Book of Romans.

The church of Christ began early to worship on the first day of the week, Sunday (Acts 20:7; 1 Cor. 16:2). No doubt many Christians of Jewish background continued to observe the traditional Saturday Sabbath as well as the Lord's Day. Paul states plainly in Romans that there was nothing wrong with that, but it certainly was not mandatory for Jewish Christians or for those of Gentile background to celebrate the Saturday Sabbath. Most likely, the issue in Rome was never whether or not the weekly Lord's Day should be kept, but simply whether or not Christians could continue to celebrate the Jewish holy days. Paul saw nothing wrong in Jewish Christians continuing in this practice as long as no one in the church at Rome insisted that the Jewish holy days were obligatory.

If Paul were writing to the twentieth-century American church, he most certainly would take up the *necessity* of observing the weekly Lord's Day. The weekly Sabbath means almost nothing to modern unbelievers and not much more to many Christians today. Some believers work on the Lord's Day as willingly as on any other day; others spend most of the Lord's Day in recreation or sports. Too many feel it would be legalistic and puritanical to observe the Sabbath. We are ignorant—perhaps willfully so—of the New Testament authority for the continuing validity of a weekly Sabbath devoted to rest, worship, and the contemplation of God's finished works of creation and redemption. The Sabbath was instituted in the beginning so that man might contemplate God's finished work of creation (Exod. 20:11). Israel was also commanded to observe the Sabbath in remembrance of their salvation from Egypt (Deut. 5:15). How much more cause have Christians, above and beyond the commandment, to celebrate God's finished work of redemption! We are God's new creation, his redeemed people (2 Cor. 4:6; 5:17; Gal. 6:15-16). Let us not go so far as to make Sabbath observance an essential of the faith, but let us not make it a matter of indifference!

5. Love Limits Liberty

Most of Paul's remarks in chapter 14 are addressed to the man strong in faith. This brother knows that Christ has set him free from the ceremonial law. He knows that food offered to an idol is clean; no matter what the heathen worshiper intends, the earth is the Lord's and everything in it (Ps. 24:1; 1 Cor. 10:26). He knows that wine is not evil in itself though the abuse of alcohol is terrible. He knows that he is free to celebrate the weekly Sabbath on the Lord's Day; he is also free (if he is a Jewish Christian) to continue to celebrate the Jewish holy days, aware now of how the truths they foreshadow have been fulfilled in Christ.

We may wonder why Paul does not seek to convince the weaker brother of his liberty in Christ. Why doesn't he take this opportunity to correct the imperfect view of the less mature Christians in Rome? Why does he instead direct most of chapter 14 to the brother who rejoices in his liberty in Christ, the man strong in faith?

Paul's chief concern is the spiritual well-being of the Christians in Rome (1:5-6,11-12). The greatest danger to their spiritual well-being was not the immaturity of young Christians. Paul knew that in time God would bring them to a fuller understanding of the gospel and of Christian freedom (Eph. 1:15-19; Phil. 1:6,9-11; Col. 1:9-10). The great danger was, rather, that those weak in faith might sin against their consciences and make shipwreck of their faith before they grew into a mature understanding of Christian liberty (1 Tim. 1:19). Sin, not ignorance or immaturity, was the great danger to believers in Rome. It is the greatest danger we face today. Paul was aware that the strong in faith could increase the danger we face today. Paul was aware that the strong in faith could increase the danger of sin for others, and for this reason he directs chapter 14 primarily to the strong in faith.

How can those strong in faith harm the weak? They can harm them by the open practice of conduct the weaker believers consider sinful. The example of the more mature brother may move the weaker Christian to engage in the same behavior before having the faith to believe that the practice under consideration is acceptable to God. The weaker brother may be halfway convinced by the stronger Christian's example, but to be halfway convinced is still to doub; nd to engage in behavior about which one has doubts is sin (verse 23). Without denying that God preserves his elect and keeps them from falling away entirely from Christ, we still must acknowledge that we can gravely wound a brother or sister and damage the church by our example. The danger is not that a genuine Christian can lose his or her salvation. Paul gave us ample assurance in chapters 5 and 8 that those whom Christ foreknew, predestined, called, and justified in love while they were his enemies will be preserved and glorified with Christ now that they are his friends (5:5b-10; 8:28-29). It is rather that the weaker Christian's walk with God, sense of peace and personal fellowship with God, and growth in Christ will be destroyed. The doubt and sense of guilt for transgressing his own conscience will wreak unhappiness and anguish of spirit.

For the stronger Christian the demands of love are clear: he must refrain from behavior that could damage the faith of the less mature brother or lead him to sin against his conscience. If eating meat is the problem, the stronger brother should not eat meat in the presence of the weaker brother. The twentieth-century Christian will be able to think of contemporary issues involving the same principle (see answer to study question 9, 14:1-23, in Appendix B).

What about my Christian liberty? Am I to restrict my freedom in Christ because of the mistaken views of a younger Christian? *Absolutely*—unless the weaker brother seeks to impose his imperfect, false understanding on the whole church. I can refrain from open practice of what is good to me out of love for my brother with joy and confidence. I can be confident that in time God will lead my brother into a more mature understanding of the truth. When the church functions as it ought, when unity and peace and love prevail among the members of the body, then each believer will grow in knowledge and faith through the exercise of the gifts of the Holy Spirit. That is God's pattetrn for the church (12:3-13; 1 Cor. 12:22-26; Eph. 4:1-16). But when I contribute toward my brother's fall into sin by stubbornly insisting on my rights, then both his grtowth and mine come to a halt. Inded, I find myself to be a sinner by spurning the law of love (13:8-10).

LESSON 18
Romans 15:1-33

STUDY QUESTIONS
1. What principles should govern our behavior toward our fellow believers? (15:1-2, 5, 7-8)

2. How did Jesus illustrate and exemplify these principles? (15:3-8; see also Matt. 12:20)

3. Paul quotes Psalm 69:7-9 in verse 3. What is the significance of this verse for Paul's argument?

4. What enables us to glorify God together? (15:5-6)

5. Why should we accept each other? (15:7)

6. What is Paul's purpose in quoting the Old Testament in verses 8-13? What is the function of those quotations in his argument?

7. Paul has a high view of the knowledge and maturity of the Christians in Rome. Why then does he write such a long doctrinal letter to them? (15:14-15; also 1:11-12; 16:17-19)

8. What were Paul's goals as a minister of Christ? (15:16, 19, 20)

9. What were Paul's means in proclaiming the gospel? (15:18-19; see also 1 Cor. 1:17; 2:1-5)

10. How much of the task that God had given him had Paul completed at the time he wrote Romans? (15:22-24)

11. What work remained for Paul to accomplish? (15:24-28)

12. How could the Christians at Rome be Paul's co-workers? (15:24-33)

STUDY NOTES

1. Christ Our Example

Verses 1-7 of chapter 15 continue the thought of chapter 14. Paul exhorts us in chapter 14 to accept each other and to defer to our brother's scruples out of love. He reinforces this exhortation in Romans 15 by appealing to the example of Christ. We should please our neighbor rather than ourselves because Christ lived to please the Father rather than himself (Luke 22:42; John 5:30; 6:38). Christ prayed for the unity of his disciples (John 17:11, 22-23); we should endeavor to maintain the unity he desires. We should welcome all who call on the name of Jesus Christ, for Christ welcomed all of us into his fellowship. Christ became a servant to his Jewish kinsmen; we should serve our brothers also. If love for our fellow Christians is not sufficient motivation to accept them and even to defer to their scruples on nonessential matters, the desire to follow our Savior's example certainly should be cause enough.

2. God's Acceptance of the Gentiles

The greatest example of welcoming the unwelcome was Christ's acceptance of the Gentiles into his people. The earliest Christians, who were all Jews, found this surprising at first (Acts 11:6; 15:14). Paul has dealt with the universal character of sin and salvation through faith throughout Romans. He reintroduces the theme of God's gracious reception of the Gentiles in verses 7-13 for two reasons.

First, Paul shows that Christ secured the eternal salvation of the Gentiles by doing God's will rather than pleasing himself. We are to follow the Lord's example. We help the weaker brother grow spiritually by having more regard for his good than for our own rights and pleasures. We also help the church increase and grow by accepting the weaker brother, just as God's ingathering of the Gentiles brings the worldwide church nearer to its intended fullness. God has room in the church for "the poor, the crippled, the blind and the lame" (Luke 14:21). If we are to "make them come in" (Luke 14:23), we certainly must welcome them once they have entered. After all, most of us were "Gentile sinners" (Gal. 2:15) and salvation is of the Jews (John 4:22), yet Christ welcomed us.

Secondly, Paul reintroduces the theme of the salvation of the Gentiles, because he intends to conclude his letter with a review of his past ministry to the Gentiles and a preview of what he hopes to accomplish in the future.

3. Paul's Ministry: Past and Future

Paul was proud of what he had accomplished for Christ. He claimed to have "fully proclaimed" the gospel in the entire eastern Mediterranean world from Jerusalem to the region of Illyricum on the Adriatic coast of today's Yugoslavia. How could he make such a claim? The Book of Acts describes Paul's missionary journeys. By tracing them on a map one can determine that they hardly covered the region "from Jerusalem all the way around to Illyricum" (15:19). Acts gives no account of Paul's ever having visited Illyricum; most likely, he never came closer to Illyricum than Macedonia and Achaia, which together constitute modern Greece.

However, Paul had planted churches in key provincial and regional centers: Paphos in Cyprus; Iconium, Lystra, and Derbe in Galatia; Antioch in Pisidia; Perga in Pamphylia; various unnamed churches in Syria and Cilicia; Troas in Mysia; Philippi, Berea, and Thessalonica in Macedonia; Athens and Corinth in Achaia, and Ephesus in Asia (i.e., western Turkey). These churches were self-governing, with their own elders (also called bishops) to rule them; they had their own pastors, teachers, evangelists, and others gifted by the Holy Spirit for the edification and growth of the churches and the spread of the gospel (see 12:1-21, note 3). Paul had founded churches that would reach out into their surrounding regions and proclaim Christ in the neighboring cities, towns, and villages. He was confident that even Illyricum, which he apparently had never visited, would be penetrated by evangelists (and ordinary Christians as well) from Macedonia and Achaia and, perhaps, also from Italy, where others had carried the gospel.

History proved Paul right. The whole eastern Mediterranean world was saturated with the gospel message and populated with churches at an early date. There was no work remaining for an apostle to do in those parts. But Spain! This was unevangelized territory unlikely to be reached by evangelists from existing churches for many decades—and that was where Paul wanted to go next.

Paul's heart is best revealed, perhaps, by contrast with the prophet Jonah. The land Paul knew as Spain was the Tarshish of Jonah's day. Jonah sought to *avoid* taking the Word of the Lord to the heathen of Nineveh by taking a ship for Tarshish. He thought of Tarshish as the end of the world, a country God did not even notice, a backwater where he could escape from the presence of the Lord (Jonah 1:1-3). Paul, on the other hand, wanted to go to Spain (the end of the Roman world) for just the opposite reason: he burned to declare the Word of God to the heathen. He knew that God was the God of Spain also, having a people of his own in Spain prepared to respond in faith to the gospel of Jesus Christ.

Paul expected the church at Rome to help him on his way to Spain with hospitality, perhaps also with money or traveling companions. He assumed that the believers there wanted to share in the work of evangelizing the ends of the earth. We need Paul's vision for the lost, for those far away as well as those near at hand. May we seek ways to share in the work of spreading the gospel in our day: by furnishing men and women, by supplying funds, and by praying with and for our missionaries.

Romans 16:1-27

1. Who was Phoebe, and what was her relationship to Paul and to the church at Rome? (16:1-2)

2. Who were Priscilla and Aquila? (16:3-5; see also Acts 18:1-4)

3. Was Paul personally acquainted with all those he greets in verses 3-15?

4. What is Paul's warning to the church at Rome? (16:17-20)

5. Why do some persons create divisions in the church and teach false doctrine? (16:18; see also 1 Tim. 6:3-5; Titus 1:10-11)

6. How can the church ward off divison and error? (16:17b, 19-20, 25)

7. Paul writes in verses 25-26 of "the revelation of the mystery hidden for long ages past, but now revealed and made known through the prophetic writings by the command of the eternal God, so that all nations might believe and obey him."

   a. What is "the mystery hidden for long ages past"? (see also Eph. 1:9-10; Col. 1:25-27)

   b. How has the mystery been "revealed and made known through the prophetic writings by the command of the eternal God"?

STUDY NOTES

1. Phoebe: Servant or Deaconess?

Phoebe is described in 16:1 as a *diakonos* of the church in Cenchrea. The Greek word *diakonos* means *servant* or, more precisely, one who *ministers to* or *waits upon* his master to do his bidding. Sometimes in the New Testament *diakonos* is also used in a technical sense to refer to a *deacon*. The apostles ordained the first deacons and charged them with meeting the material needs of the poor in the Jerusalem church (Acts 6:1-6). (Although the word *diakonos* is not used in Acts 6:1-6, the related words *diakonia*, translated *distribution* or *minstry*, and *diakonein*, translated *to wait on*, are found in 6:1, 2, 4.) The office of deacon spread quickly to the churches in other localities. By the time Paul was writing his letters, local churches were selecting their own elders and deacons (Phil. 1:1; 1 Tim. 3:8-13). Was Phoebe a deaconess or was she an unordained servant of the church?

Paul lists the qualities of elders and deacons in 1 Timothy 3:8-13. He declares that a deacon must be a man worthy of respect (3:8), with but one wife (3:2) who must also be worthy of respect (3:11). Based on this passage of Scripture, evangelical churches historically have held that deacons must be men.

Some writers and some evangelical churches of the present day contest the proposition that a woman may not occupy the office of deacon. They cite Romans 16:1 as evidence that women occupied that office in the early church. Their argument, however, is without merit. If women were eligible for ordination to the office of deacon, Paul certainly would have made this clear in 1 Timothy 3:8-13. The passage in 1 Timothy is a *didactic* portion of Scripture, i.e., a passage that presents systematic teaching on a subject. On the other hand, Romans 16:1 is an *incidental* passage regarding the diaconate. Paul's intention in 16:1-2 is to commend Phoebe to the care of the church in Rome; only in passing does he refer to her as a *diakonos*. It is a cardinal rule of biblical *hermeneutics* (the science of interpretation) that didactic passages serve to illuminate the meaning of incidental passages, not vice versa. We must conclude that Phoebe was not a deaconess, but, rather, an unordained servant of the church in Cenchrea.

We dare not lose sight of the fact that Paul's purpose in 16:1-2 is to commend Phoebe for her faithful service and to call on the Christians in Rome to honor and assist her. Although women are not eligible for the *offices* of elder and deacon, both men and women receive the *gift* of service—*diakonia* in the general sense of the word—for the benefit of the whole church (12:7). All who have the gift of service are to exercise their gift, and all of God's servants are to be honored by us for their faithfulness. The experience of countless churches shows that many women are of greater service to the church than some men who occupy the office of deacon. Indeed, the women and not the men are the backbone of some churches. The women in such congregations are to be honored for their faithfulness, but what of the men who are shirking their God-given responsibilities? Male or female, church officer or not, each Christian is to be "a servant of the church" as Phoebe was. May we receive a commendation from the Lord for our faithfulness like the one Paul accords Phoebe for hers!

2. Paul's Co-Workers

In addition to Phoebe, Paul commends Priscilla (or Prisca) and Aquila, Mary, Urbanus, Tryphaena, Tryphosa, and Persis for their work for the Lord. Priscilla, Aquila, and Urbanus had worked with Paul personally; perhaps some of the others also had been with him on his travels. A careful reading of Acts reveals that Paul was not a solitary missionary lacking companions or support from other believers. On the contrary, he always had traveling companions to share the gospel work. He accepted lodging and food in towns where he labored, and he may have received some financial backing from the church in Antioch, which sent him out at first (Acts 13:1-3). Paul was able to refuse any material help from the Corinthian church while he lived and worked there, only because Christians elsewhere in Macedonia and Achaia supplemented the income he derived from his trade (1 Cor. 9:12-15; 2 Cor. 11:7-9).

Our missionaries and "full-time Christian workers" think of us as their co-workers. Without our prayers, encouragement, financial help, and hospitality they would be far less free and able to carry out the ministry God has given them. For us, being co-workers with those exercising the gifts of preaching, teaching, evangelism, and medical healing on a full-time basis (whether at home or abroad) is an essential part of becoming living sacrifices for Christ (12:1-2). To live for God requires that we view ourselves as part of a single body with different parts that need each other—parts that all must function properly if the body is to glorify Christ and carry out his work in the world (12:1-13). We see again that all of the Book of Romans from chapter 13 on is based on the principles of chapter 12.

3. Doctrine and Divisions

What are the sources of conflict and division in the church? Are you surprised to learn that true doctrine is an occasion for division? The personal motivation of someone who creates strife may be satisfaction of the desires of the old nature, such as love of money or pride (16:18), but the issue at stake is often the emergence of teaching contrary to sound doctrine (16:17). The churches that care most about maintaining pure doctrine are those that experience the most strife and division! Those believers who maintain that what a church teaches and believes is important, whether they be a majority or a minority in the church, will not allow false doctrine to spread silently. On the other hand, denominations with few who care much about doctrine are seldom troubled by divisions; they are also seldom blessed with sound teaching. False doctrine *will* arise. The question is, What will be the reaction of the church?

Divisions are not likely to arise when the church does not know pure doctrine or cares but little to maintain it. However, one of two things will happen whenever there are those in the church who believe that doctrine is important enough to fight for. Those in error will be forced to leave if those who adhere to the truth constitute a majority, or those who hold to true doctrine may be forced out if they are a minority. There is always sin on someone's part when divisions occur, but divisions on doctrinal matters also reveal spiritual health (1 Cor. 11:19; 1 John 2:18-20). It is healthy that some care enough for the truth to fight for it.

Paul writes to remind the Roman church of the major doctrines of the faith so that they will be able to recognize heresy when it appears. He urges them to isolate and shun false teachers when they are recognized, nipping the growth of false doctrine in the bud (verses 17, 20). For centuries the church in Rome did remain pure in doctrine, in spite of persecution from without and heresies in the church elsewhere in the empire. Only when the church at Rome faced no obvious threats to its life and teaching and, perhaps, ceased to be vigilant for the truth did it go astray in doctrine.

We may believe our churches are pure in doctrine. If so, let us strive to keep them that way. To do so, our church must first of all ensure that all its members, adults as well as youth and children, are thoroughly taught the basic truths of the faith. Then, we must periodically remind ourselves of the truth we know, just as Paul reminded the church at Rome. Finally, we must pass on to our children both true doctrine and a love of the same.

4. The Mystery of the Gospel Revealed

The mystery of the gospel (16:25) is no special teaching for the inner circle of the church, no doctrine reserved for the spiritual or intellectual elite. The mystery of the gospel has been revealed to all. It is simply the truth that God saves Jew and Gentile in the same way—through faith in Jesus Christ. Salvation is not by works of the law, whether delivered to the Jews in written form or known in the hearts of all men; salvation is through faith in the work of Christ for us. When we trust in Jesus Christ, believing that what he did in living and dying was for us and for our sins, God justifies us and gives us new life in Christ. God has chosen a people for himself from both the Jews and the Gentiles. Day by day, heart by heart, God is grafting an innumerable multitude of Jews and Gentiles into his spiritual people Israel, the church of Christ. There is but one gospel, one way of salvation for all mankind. It is the gospel that Paul sets forth so clearly in Romans. The mystery of the gospel is a mystery no more!

Yet the gospel is still a mystery to most of our friends and neighbors, to most of the world. They do not know the way of salvation. We know it. The smallest child who trusts in Jesus knows enough of what once was a mystery to be saved. Since we know the truth of salvation while our friends and relations and neighbors do not, what is our responsibility? What ought we to do?

The Christian who has completed this study should be able to open the Bible to the Book of Romans and go through Paul's great letter point by point, explaining the truths of the gospel. He or she should be able to show in Romans what is false about the common errors so widespread even in our supposedly Christian lands. God grant that the Christian who has completed this study will be burdened to share the truth of the gospel with others and will be confident that he or she can do so from Romans.

APPENDIX A
Romans Review

STUDY QUESTIONS

1. Outline Romans.
2. List the important themes or topics of Romans.
3. Prepare an outline of the plan of salvation based on Romans that you could use to share the gospel with a friend.

1. OUTLINE OF ROMANS

Introduction
1:1-7	Greeting
1:8-15	Paul's ministry
1:16-17	Theme: The gospel is the power of God for salvation; it is God's righteousness in Christ for those who believe.

Sin and Guilt
1:18-32	Man's sin and God's wrath
2:1-29	Individual guilt; God's impartiality toward Jew and Gentile
3:1-20	Excuses refuted; all proved guilty

Justification Through Faith
3:21-31	God's righteousness through faith in Christ for all who believe
4:1-25	The example of Abraham

Assurance
5:1-11	God's abiding love
5:12-21	The work of Christ greater than that of Adam

Freedom from Sin
6:1-23	Identification with Christ: Dead to sin, alive to God
7:1-4	Identification with Christ: Dead to law
7:5-25	The power of the sinful nature
8:1-4a	Identification with Christ: No condemnation
8:4b-17	Life in the Spirit; sons of God
8:18-39	The keeping power of God

God's Purpose in History

9:1-33	The sovereignty of God in election
10:1-21	Israel has rejected righteousness through faith
11:1-24	Israel's remnant and the salvation of the Gentiles
11:25-36	The accomplishment of God's sovereign purpose: All Israel will be saved.

Christian Living

12:1-21	How to think and how to live: In the church and in the world
13:1-14	The Christian and the state
14:1–15:13	Christian liberty and the weaker brother

Conclusion

15:14-33	Paul's ministry to the Gentiles; his future plans
16:1-27	Greetings to individuals; warning against false teachers; benediction

2. IMPORTANT THEMES IN ROMANS

Natural knowledge of God (1:18-20, 32; 2:14-15)

Universal guilt (1:18-32)

God's righteous principles of judgment (2:5-16)

Individual guilt (2:1-3, 17-24; 3:9-20)

Justification through faith and the work of Christ (1:16-17; 3:21-31)

One way of salvation for all mankind (3:19-23, 29-30; 4:1-11)

Assurance of salvation (5:1-21; 8:1-4, 9-39)

Dead to sin and alive to God (6:1-13; 8:10-13)

Dead to the law (6:14–7:6)

The old nature and the struggle against sin (7:7-25)

Life in the Spirit (8:1-17)

Assurance in adversity (8:18-39)

The sovereignty of God in election (9:1-33; 11:11-36)

God has one people, Israel, containing both Jews and Gentiles (11:11-36)

Living sacrifices for God (12:1-21)

Gifts of the Spirit (12:4-8)

The Christian and government (13:1-7)

Christian liberty and the weaker brother (14:1–15:7)

Adiaphora: indifferent practices (14:1-23)

Co-workers in the gospel ministry (15:24–16:16)

3. GOD'S PLAN OF SALVATION

The Gospel in a Nutshell: Romans 1:16-17

I am not ashamed of the gospel, because it is the power of God for the salvation of everyone who believes: first for the Jew, then for the Gentile. For in the gospel a righteousness from God is revealed, a righteousness that is by faith from first to last, just as it is written: "The righteous will live by faith."

I.   All Are Sinners and Under the Condemnation of God
A.   Romans 2:1-3

You, therefore, have no excuse, you who pass judgment on someone else, for at whatever point you judge the other, you are condemning yourself, because you who pass judgment do the same things. Now we know that God's judgment against those who do such things is based on truth. So when you, a mere man, pass judgment on them and yet do the same things, do you think you will escape God's judgment?

B. *Romans 3:9-10*

What shall we conclude then? Are we any better? Not at all! We have already made the charge that Jews and Gentiles alike are all under sin. As it is written: "There is no one righteous, not even one. . . ."

C. *Romans 3:23*

. . . for all have sinned and fall short of the glory of God.

II. God Hates Sin

A. *Romans 1:18*

The wrath of God is being revealed from heaven against all the godlessness and wickedness of men who suppress the truth by their wickedness. . . .

B. *Romans 1:32*

Although they know God's righteous decree that those who do such things deserve death, they not only continue to do these very things but also approve of those who practice them.

C. *Romans 2:5*

But because of your stubbornness and your unrepentant heart, you are storing up wrath against yourself for the day of God's wrath, when his righteous judgment will be revealed.

III. No Excuses

A. *Romans 2:11-13*

For God does not show favoritism. All who sin apart from the law will also perish apart from the law, and all who sin under the law will be judged by the law. For it is not those who hear the law who are righteous in God's sight, but it is those who obey the law who will be declared righteous.

B. *Romans 3:19*

Now we know that whatever the law says, it says to those who
are under the law, so that every mouth may be silenced and the
whole world held accountable to God.

IV. *Salvation Through Faith in Christ*
A. *Romans 1:3-4*

. . . regarding his Son, who as to his human nature was a
descendant of David, and who through the Spirit of holiness
was declared with power to be the Son of God by his resurrection from the dead: Jesus Christ our Lord.

B. *Romans 3:21-25a*

But now, a righteousness from God, apart from law, has been
made known, to which the Law and the prophets testify. This
righteousness from God comes through faith in Jesus Christ to
all who believe. There is no difference, for all have sinned and
fall short of the glory of God, and are justified freely by his grace
through the redemption that came by Christ Jesus. God presented him as a sacrifice of atonement, through faith in his
blood.

C. *Romans 4:24-25*

. . . for us, to whom God will credit righteousness—for us who
believe in him who raised Jesus our Lord from the dead. He was
delivered over to death for our sins and was raised to life for our
justification.

D. *Romans 10:9-11, 13*

That if you confess with your mouth, "Jesus is Lord," and
believe in your heart that God raised him from the dead, you
will be saved. For it is with your heart that your believe and are
justified, and it is with your mouth that you confess and are
saved. . . . the same Lord is Lord of all and richly blesses all
who call on him, for "Everyone who calls on the name of the
Lord will be saved."

V. Assurance

A. *Romans 5:1*

Therefore, since we have been justified through faith, we have peace with God through our Lord Jesus Christ.

B. *Romans 5:8-9*

But God demonstrates his own love for us in this: While we were still sinners, Christ died for us. Since we have now been justified by his blood, how much more shall we be saved from God's wrath through him. For if, when we were God's enemies, we were reconciled to him through the death of his Son, how much more, having been reconciled, shall we be saved through his life!

C. *Romans 8:1*

Therefore, there is now no condemnation for those who are in Christ Jesus, because through Christ Jesus the law of the Spirit of life set me free from the law of sin and death.

APPENDIX B

Answers to Study Questions

LESSON 1: ROMANS 1:1-17

1. What does Paul say about himself? (1:1)

Paul states that he is: (a) A *servant* of Christ Jesus. The Greek word translated *servant* is *doulos*, better translated *slave*. (b) Called to be an apostle. The word *apostle* comes directly from the Greek *apostolos*, meaning a *messenger* or one sent forth under orders. (c) Set apart for the gospel of God.

2. What does he say about the gospel? (1:1-3)

(a) It is *God's* gospel (not Paul's own message). (b) It was promised beforehand by God through his prophets in the Scriptures, i.e., the Old Testament. (c) The gospel is the good tidings concerning God's Son. The Greek word translated *gospel* is *euangelion*, derived from the Greek prefix for *good* plus the word for *message* or tidings.

3. What does he say about Jesus Christ? (1:3-4)

(a) As regards his human nature Jesus is a descendant of King David. (b) As regards his divine nature Jesus is the Son of God. The proof of his divinity, or God-nature, was his resurrection from the dead. (c) Jesus is our Lord. The Greek word translated *Lord* is *kurios*; it means *he to whom a person belongs; one's master; one's God.*

4. What is Jesus Christ's relationship to Paul? (1:4-5)

(a) Jesus Christ is Paul's *Lord* (see Acts 9:5). (b) Paul received grace and apostleship through Jesus Christ. *Grace* is favor or something good given freely, without respect to the worthiness of the recipient. Apostleship was part of God's grace to Paul. In sending Paul forth as an apostle the Lord favored him with authority and responsibility much greater than he deserved.

5. What is Paul's relationship to the Christians in Rome? (1:6-7, 8-10)
   (a) They, like Paul, have been called to belong to Christ. (b) Paul and his readers have a common Father and a common Lord. (c) Paul always prays for them. (d) Paul wants to visit them.

6. Give four reasons why Paul wants to visit Rome. (1:11-15)
   (a) He wants to impart some spiritual gift to the Christians in Rome to build up and strengthen their faith. (b) He wants to receive encouragement from them; i.e., he expects his own faith to be strengthened by his visit. (c) He expects to reap a spiritual harvest in Rome; i.e., he hopes to convert more Gentiles there to Christ. (d) Paul is obligated to all men. God commissioned him to bring the gospel to the Gentiles everywhere, including Rome.

7. What is Paul's attitude towards his task? Why does he have this attitude? (1:14-16)
   (a) Paul is obligated, eager, and unashamed to preach in Rome. (b) Paul is *unashamed* (not hesitant, reticent, or at a loss for words when contemplating preaching in proud Rome) because of the *power* of the gospel: the gospel is the power of God for salvation.

8. What is the theme of the gospel? (1:16-17; see also 1:2-3)
   The theme of the gospel is *the righteousness of God*, which is *the power of God for salvation*.

9. How is the gospel message made known to us? (1:17)
   God has *revealed* the gospel. The gospel is not something we come to know or discover for ourselves by reason, experience, or discussion. God made it known by Christ and his apostles, and we find their message in the Scriptures. God inspired the Scriptures such that they are a complete, trustworthy, and error-free record of God's revelation (see 2 Tim. 3:15-16).

10. How do we receive the righteousness of God revealed in the gospel? (1:17)

We make the gospel and all that it promises our own by *faith*, i.e., by *believing* what God has said and by *trusting* in Jesus Christ, in whom is found the righteousness of God revealed in the gospel.

LESSON 2: ROMANS 1:18–2:16

1. What do we need to be saved from? (1:18, 32)

(a) We need to be saved from the wrath of God. (b) We need to be saved from death, which is the penalty we deserve for our sins.

2. What is the cause of God's wrath against mankind? (1:18-21)

The cause of God's wrath is the wickedness and godlessness of men; in particular, their conscious suppression of the truths that God exists, is powerful and glorious, and is worthy of praise.

3. How has God revealed himself to men? Has he revealed himself to all men? What has he revealed of himself? (1:19-20)

(a) God has revealed himself in and through creation. (b) He has indeed revealed himself to all mankind, for the created world is present to all. (c) In creation God has revealed his eternal power and divine nature (i.e., his deity or Godhead).

4. How ought man to respond to God's revelation of himself? How has he responded? (1:21-23)

(a) Man ought to glorify God and thank him for his person and for his goodness in creating such a world as ours and putting us in it. (b) Man's response to God's revelation of himself in creation has been to refuse to glorify God or to thank him. He has instead glorified and worshiped the creation in place of the Creator.

5. What has God done to punish man's rejection of him (1:24-31)

God has given mankind over to: (a) sinful desires (1:24); (b) unnatural, shameful lusts (1:26); (c) a depraved mind (1:28); (d) all sorts of evil practices (1:29-31).

6. Has God's giving men over to sin and depravity served to bring them to repentance? Was it intended to do so? *(1:32)*

(a) God's action in giving men over to their sins and the hurtful consequences of them has not brought them to repentance. (b) This passage gives no indication that the suffering, hardship, and heartbreak resulting from a life of sin in the midst of a sinful people were intended to bring men to repentance. These verses indicate that God's hardening of men in their sins is punishment—the wrath of God inflicted on sinful men.

7. Some think they will escape the condemnation falling on others. On what grounds do they deceive themselves? *(2:1-4)*

Some believe they will escape judgment because they agree with God in condemning sin—in others. Others misinterpret his patience toward mankind by rashly concluding that he never intends to punish the world.

8. Is the expression of God's wrath against sinful mankind limited to the things mentioned in 1:24-32? What more is there to the wrath of God? *(2:5)*

There is more to the expression of God's wrath than his act of hardening men in their sins in this present life. God has a day of judgment awaiting the wicked at the end of this present evil age.

9. How would you summarize God's principles of judgment? *(2:2, 5-11)*

(a) God's judgment rightly falls upon mankind, i.e., they deserve his judgment (2:2). (b) His judgment is righteous and just; everyone will get what he deserves (2:5). (c) God will give each person rewards or punishment according to what he has done, i.e., according to his works: (1) He will give eternal life, honor, glory, and peace to everyone who continues to do good (2:7, 10). (2) He will subject the disobedient, wicked, and selfish to wrath, fury, tribulation, and distress (2:8-9). (d) God's judgment is impartial: he will judge everyone, Jew and Gentile, by the same principles and standards. He shows no favoritism (2:11).

10. On what basis will God judge those who never knew the law of Moses? (2:12-15)

They will be judged on the basis of the law of God written on their hearts. The essence of his law is written on every man's heart. This truth is evidenced by the fact that men's consciences warn them when they are doing wrong and reassure them when they are doing right. Ignorance of the written law of God in the Scriptures is, therefore, no excuse.

11. Will Jews (or Christians) escape condemnation just because they have God's Word and agree with the law of God found in it? (2:1-3, 13)

Mere possession of the law of Moses does not save. It is not enough to *know* the law of God. It is not even enough to *agree* with it mentally. To escape condemnation, one must *obey* it, consistently and faithfully.

12. How much does God know of what we do, of what we think in our hearts? (2:16)

God knows everything we do, say, and think; he knows the secrets of our lives. He will call us to account for our inner thoughts, motives, and desires as well as for our deeds (Matt. 5:28).

13. Is the message of judgment a preparation for the gospel or part of the gospel? (2:16)

The doctrine of the final judgment is not simply a preparation for the gospel, but part of the gospel message we are to preach (John 16:7-11, especially verse 11).

LESSON 3: ROMANS 2:17-3:20

1. On what grounds did some Jews think they would obtain God's approval and escape his judgment? (2:17-27)

(a) They were *Jews*, God's own special people (2:17). (b) They relied on the law (2:17). (c) They boasted in God (2:17; see also Ps. 96:5). (d) They knew God's will as revealed in the law, and they approved of it (2:18). (e) They had been circumcised (2:25-27). Circumcision was the rite prescribed by God as a sign of the *covenant* (pact, agreement, contractual relationship) he had made with Abraham and his descendant—he to be their God and they to be his people forever (Gen. 17:9-14).

2. *Where did such Jews go wrong in their thinking? (2:17-27)*
   (a) They did the very things they condemned in others, things they admitted were deserving of punishment. (b) They thought the physical act of circumcision automatically made them God's people regardless of their disobedience to the law.

3. *In verses 1, 3, 5, and 7 of chapter 3, various objections are raised against Paul's charge that all men, Jews included, stand condemned by God. Paraphrase those objections in your own words.*
   (a) Verse 1: Surely there is some value in being a circumcised Jew instead of a Gentile! What is it, if not exemption from judgment? (b) Verse 3: God is obligated to be faithful to his promises to us even if we are unfaithful to him. (c) Verse 5: Since God's righteousness stands out all the more gloriously against the dark background of our wickedness, it would not be just of him to inflict wrath on us. (d) Verse 7: Since God's truthfulness is shown to be all the more glorious by my false character and lies, why does he condemn me? One might even say that it is necessary for me to do evil for his goodness to be revealed in its fullness!

4. *In verses 2, 4, 6, and 8 of chapter 3, Paul answers those objections. Paraphrase his answers in your own words.*
   (a) Verse 2: There *is* much value in being a Jew. The chief benefit is that the Jews possess the written Word of God, but this makes their sinful conduct all the more reprehensible. (b) Verse 4: Of course God must prove faithful and true, even if that means that every man proves to be false! But this also means that God will always prevail and man will always be found in the wrong whenever God and man enter into judgment. (c) Verse 6: Since the Jew has already agreed that it is just of God to judge the *world*, i.e., the Gentiles (2:1), this argument cannot be sound. God could not judge the Gentiles if the objection were valid. If the argument does not hold for the Gentiles, it cannot hold for Jews either, since it does not appeal to a difference between Jews and Gentiles. (d) Verse 8: This argument leads logically to the absurd conclusion that we should *seek* to do evil so that

good may result. Paul does not dignify this argument with a reply. He pronounces the one who would dare advance such a proposition worthy of condemnation without further ado.

5. In 3:10-18 Paul quotes several Old Testament passages: Psalm 14:1-2; Isaiah 53:6; Psalm 5:9; Psalm 140:3; Psalm 10:7; Isaiah 59:7-8; Psalm 36:1. What is his purpose in quoting these verses?
These verses are addressed to Jews and they describe Jews. Paul has already declared the Gentile world to be under condemnation. Now he shows his own people to be equally guilty. Paul wants to silence *every* mouth that would dare to justify itself before God.

6. What do Jews and Gentiles have in common? (3:19)
All are guilty and exposed to the judgment of God.

7. What does the law of Moses produce? (3:20)
The law of Moses does not produce righteousness; rather, it produces personal consciousness of sin.

LESSON 4: ROMANS 3:21–31

1. What kind of righteousness can we have? (3:21)
We can have the righteousness of God.

2. What kind of righteousness can never be ours? (3:21)
We can never have a righteousness based on our own obedience to the law.

3. How and when was the righteousness of God first made known to mankind? (3:21)
The righteousness of God was first made known in the law and the prophets, i.e., in the Old Testament. It is now known in fullness in the gospel.

4. How has this righteousness of God been made available to mankind? (3:22)
God's righteousness is found in Jesus Christ.

5. How do we make this righteousness of God our own? (3:22)
We make Christ and his righteousness ours through faith in him.

6. For whom is this righteousness of God intended? (3:22-23)
God's righteousness in Christ is intended for Jews and Gentiles alike, since all have sinned and have need of it.

7. Verses 24-25 describe God's act of providing a divine righteousness for mankind. In your own words, define these characteristics of his work for us:
   a. "Justified": To be *justified* is to be acquitted of guilt and declared legally blameless. Justification is God's verdict that we are upright and righteous. Those who have been justified are entitled to all the blessings of the upright.
   b. "Freely": *Freely* does not mean that no price was paid for our justification. Jesus paid an infinite price on our behalf, laying down his life for us. *Freely* means that we personally pay or do nothing to induce God to justify us.
   c. "By his grace": God's *grace* is his loving favor and goodness toward mankind; it is the concrete expression of his good will (Luke 2:14). God was under no necessity to be gracious to us—we do not deserve his favor because of anything we have done or are—and he was not compelled to be gracious to us because of the attributes of his divine nature. God's grace is *sovereign* grace. It is entirely a matter of his will that he sent his Son to redeem us (Eph. 1:5-10).
   d. "Redemption": *Redemption* in its most general sense is the act of purchasing something or someone for one's self. In the Old Testament the term is used of the purchase of land in which one has a hereditary interest (Lev. 25:24-32; Ruth 4:3-6); but it usually refers to the ransom of an animal or person from death, slavery, or oppression (Exod. 6:6; 13:13; 21:8; Lev. 27:13; Pss. 25:22; 77:15; 130:8; Isa. 43:1; 52:3; Jer. 31:11). In the New Testament the word *redemption* (Greek: *apolutrosis*) refers to God's act of purchasing our freedom from slavery to sin and death, the blood of Christ being the price of our lives (John 8:34-36).
   e. "Sacrifice of atonement": A *sacrifice of atonement* is the death of a pure substitute in place of one who has offended and wronged God by breaking his law. The lawbreaker deserves to die (1:32). The death of the substitute fulfills the penalty incurred by the guilty

party; the sacrifice wipes out the guilt and turns aside the wrath of God. The Greek rendered *sacrifice of atonement* in the NIV is *hilasterion,* perhaps better translated as a *means of placating or appeasing God* or as *propitiation.* In the Septuagint, the Greek translation of the Old Testament used by Paul, *hilastrion* was used to translate the Hebrew word representing the covering of the ark of the covenant, the place where the blood of the sacrifice of atonement was sprinkled once a year in order to cleanse the Israelites of their sins (Lev. 16).

f. "Faith in his blood": This phrase refers to the Christian's belief and trust that the death of Christ on the cross was the sacrifice of atonement needed for his or her justification and redemption. (See Lev. 16; Heb. 9:12-15, 22; Matt. 26:28.)

8. How did God's act of providing Jesus Christ for us demonstrate his justice? (3:25-26)

God does not fully punish the sins of men in this life. Christ has not yet brought this age to a close by coming in his glory for the final judgment. To some, God's patience and mercy indicate indifference to sin and a lack of intention to punish man's rebellion and evil. They do not believe that he will keep his promise to punish all disobedience (2 Pet. 3:3-4; Acts 17:29-31). By offering and accepting his own Son as the sacrifice for our sins, God showed that the penalty for sin had to be paid.

9. Paul voices several assertions about the gospel in 3:27-31, which he has already proved or will prove later. What are these assertions?

Paul affirms that: (a) No one can boast of his obedience to the law, i.e., of the righteousness of his works (Phil. 3:3-7). (b) A man or woman is justified through faith in Jesus Christ, not by works of the law. (c) There is but one God and, so, but one way of salvation, which is for all mankind. (d) The gospel actually establishes the validity of the law (1 John 2:7-8).

LESSON 5: Romans 4:1-12

1. To whom in particular is chapter 4 addressed? (4:1)

Chapter 4 is addressed to those who claim Abraham as their

forefather (more literal translations read, "our forefather according to the flesh"), i.e., the Jews.

2. *The Jews were proud of their forefather Abraham, but of what could Abraham be proud? (4:2-3)*
Abraham had nothing to be proud of in himself—certainly not his deeds (see, e.g., Gen. 12:10-20; 16:1-6).

3. *What was Abraham's spiritual condition when he put his faith in God? (4:5; also Josh. 24:2-3)*
Abraham was *ungodly.*

4. *How are faith and righteousness related? Is our faith equivalent to our righteousness? (4:3, 5; also 3:22)*
Verses 3 and 5 would seem to indicate that faith itself is our righteousness. But comparison with 3:22 shows that faith itself is not our righteousness, but the *means* by which we receive the righteousness of Christ as our own. My faith is as imperfect as my works. It is less than a grain of mustard seed (Matt. 17:20) and is in itself no more acceptable to a holy God than my works. But the life and death of Jesus Christ were perfect and wholly acceptable to God. His life and death were on my behalf—Christ lived and died *for me.* Faith accepts and rests on the doing and dying of Christ as God's righteousness for me. In short, my faith is not my righteousness, but it is my trust in the work of Christ as my righteousness.

5. *Paul quotes David in 4:6-8 to substantiate his argument. What is Paul's point in 4:1-8, and why is David a particularly strong witness?*
Paul's main point in these verses is that God reckons or credits righteousness to a sinner wholly apart from his works. David is a compelling witness to this truth because God considered him a man after his own heart (1 Sam. 13:14), in spite of the fact that David had committed worse sins than most men, being both an adulterer and a murderer. Yet God did not count David's sins against him; rather, he accounted him righteous. Why? Because David trusted God's promises to forgive him, deliver him from danger, and exalt him (1 Sam. 17:37, 45-47; 2 Sam. 22; Pss. 31, 34, 40, and many more).

6. What was Abraham's physical condition when he put his faith in God? (4:9-10)

Abraham was uncircumcised.

7. Why does Paul call attention to the fact that Abraham was uncircumcised at the time he was justified? (4:11-12)

(a) Paul wants to reemphasize the point made earlier (2:25-29): circumcision does not justify a man. Abraham was justified by faith *before* he was circumcised; circumcision followed. It was given as a sign and seal to confirm the righteousness Abraham had received by faith. (b) Paul also wants to reemphasize another point made earlier: there is one way of salvation for all men, uncircumcised Gentiles as well as circumcised Jews (3:22,29-30). All can follow Abraham's example of faith just as they are, without submitting to circumcision or becoming Jews first (Acts 15:5-11). Like Abraham, all can be justified by faith in God's promises fulfilled in Christ.

LESSON 6: ROMANS 4:13-25

1. What did Abraham receive as a result of having the righteousness that comes through faith? (4:13)

Abraham received a promise from God that he would inherit the world (Gen. 17:4-8; 18:18). That promise was also made to his descendants, and they would likewise receive the promised blessing through faith.

2. What ensures us that the promise is still valid? (4:14-16)

The promise rests entirely on God's grace and not on man's works. It is given to those who through faith in Christ alone are reckoned righteous. If keeping the law were the condition for receiving the promised blessing, then the promise would be null and void. The law brings only wrath, for no one keeps the law.

3. How can Gentile believers in Jesus know that they will receive the promise made to Abraham? (4:16-17)

They share in the blessing of Abraham because they, as believers in Christ, are true descendants and heirs of Abraham (Gal. 3:26-29).

4. In what kind of God did Abraham believe, and what did he believe God could do? (4:17)

Abraham believed in a God who could bring the dead to life. First of all, he believed that God could bring life to Sarah's womb and give him the son he had promised. Later, when God commanded him to slay Isaac (the promised son) on an altar, Abraham believed that God would raise his son from the dead (Heb. 11:17-19).

5. How is Abraham's faith like our own? (Compare verses 17 and 24.)

In the case of his son Isaac, Abraham believed that God could raise the dead. We believe that God did raise Christ from the dead. Perhaps Abraham even knew that God would raise Christ from the dead, for Jesus affirmed that Abraham rejoiced to see his (Christ's) day (John 8:56).

6. Compare Genesis 17:17-18 with Romans 4:19-20. How can Paul claim that Abraham did not waver through unbelief?

The full context of the passage containing Genesis 17:17-18 reveals that Abraham obeyed God by submitting to circumcision (Gen. 17:9-14, 22-27). The act of circumcision for him was an act of faith in the promise of God. God did not judge Abraham's doubts or wavering through unbelief. Abraham's *actions* showed his underlying faith. Our faith is shown by our works (James 2:14-26, especially verse 18).

7. What does the death of Christ have to do with our salvation? (4:25)

Christ was put to death for our sins. His blood was the penalty required by God (3:25; also Isa. 53:4-5; Heb. 9:25-28).

8. What does the resurrection of Christ have to do with our justification? (4:25)

(a) If Christ was not raised, then his death did not suffice for us and we are still in our sins (1 Cor. 15:17). But his death *did* cleanse us from our sins; he *did* complete his work of redemption. Having completed his work, Christ could be, indeed, had to be raised from the dead (Acts 2:24). (b) As the risen Lord to whom all judgment has been committed (John 5:21-30), Christ will pronounce our verdict of justification on the last day. Indeed, he has already proclaimed that verdict in heaven. There is no longer any place left there for Satan, the accuser of our brothers and sisters (Rev. 12:9-11). The risen Christ pleads continuously before God on our behalf (1 John 2:1)

LESSON 7: ROMANS 5:1–21

1. What is the ground of our assurance that we will remain at peace with God? What is the basis of our peace with God? (5:1-2)

(a) We have been justified through faith in Christ. We will remain at peace with God as long as we continue to trust Christ, for the basis of our justification is the work of Christ and not our own works. (b) Through Christ, we have entered the sphere of God's special favor (grace). God's grace rests on his Son (Matt. 3:17; Mark 9:7; John 1:17), and all who are in him stand in God's grace. This is the basis of our peace with God.

2. What hope does this assurance bring? (5:2; see also Dan. 12:2-3)

We have the hope of sharing the glory of God. (See also 1:23; 2:7, 10; 2:23; John 17:5, 24; Col. 1:27; 2 Thess. 2:14; 2 Pet. 1:3.)

3. It is natural to rejoice in our hope for the future, but we can even rejoice in present suffering. Tell how suffering now produces hope for the future (5:3-4).

Tribulation and suffering produce patience, steadfastness, and endurance in us. As we continue to endure, we realize that our very endurance is proof that our faith is real. (Or, possibly, our endurance creates *character* [Greek: *dokime*] that is seen to be tested and approved by God. The word *dokime* can mean *approval, tested character,* or *proof* itself.) Such proof or character gives us reason to hope for the future (see James 1:2-3).

4. What keeps our hope strong in spite of continued suffering? How can we be sure that we will endure through thick and thin? (5:5)

Our hope remains strong because of the love of God poured out into our hearts by the Holy Spirit. This love of God in our hearts that Paul has in mind is probably the Spirit-inspired assurance that God will continue to keep us in the circle of *his* love (5:6-10ff.) rather than *our* love for God that the Holy Spirit generates in us.

5. Summarize Paul's words of encouragement in 5:6-10.

We can be confident that God will not let us slip away from him now that we belong to him. God loved us enough to send his Son to die for us when we were his enemies. Now we are reconciled to him—his friends, abiding in the sphere of his saving grace. We have all the more reason now to believe that he loves us and will preserve us as his own.

6. Paul rejoices in three things as a result of our justification. What are those three things? (5:2-11)

He rejoices in our hope of sharing the glory of God (5:2), in our sufferings (5:3), and in God himself (5:11).

7. How did the sin of Adam affect us? (5:12-19)

The trespass of Adam made all men sinners (5:12, 19), resulting in the condemnation (5:16,18) and death (5:15,17) of all. Note: Paul uses the terms "all men" (5:12,18) and "the many" (5:15,19) synonymously and interchangeably (compare the parallel verses).

8. In 5:13-14 Paul offers proof for his assertion that we suffer the consequences of Adam's first sin. Summarize his argument.

The fact that *all* die proves that God holds *all* to be guilty of sin, since death is the result of sin (6:23; also Gen. 2:17; 3:3). Sin is disobedience to the law of God (1 John 3:4). During the time from Adam to Moses men did not possess the law of God in verbal form. (Abraham was probably an exception; Gen. 18:19; 26:5.) Personal sin is not counted against those who have no law to transgress (4:15), yet all die, even those who are not personally transgressors. Paul concludes that the universal reign of sin must be attributed to a greater cause than the personal sins of men and women. In fact, all die because of *Adam's* transgression. His act made sinners of us all, because Adam, like Christ, was a representative of the many. (See 5:1-21, note 5 for a fuller discussion of verses 13-14.)

9. How was Adam a "pattern" (5:14) of Christ? (5:15-19)

Adam's actions *affected* all. Even more, Adam was a *representative* of the many. What he did was done on behalf of and imputed to all his descendants.

10. *How was Christ's act of redemption greater than Adam's act of transgression? (5:15-19)*

The grace of God in Christ has abounded *much more* than the sin and death that abounded through Adam (5:15, 20). Justification based on Christ's righteousness is greater than condemnation based on many acts of unrighteousness (5:16, 18). The grace and righteousness that are ours in Christ ensure that we will reign in eternal life much more than death has reigned in this world through sin (5:17).

11. *Why did God give Israel the law? (5:20)*

God gave the law so that *trespasses*—sins against a known standard— might multiply. But God had a purpose in letting sin multiply: he intended to make his grace multiply all the more in Jesus Christ (see 7:7-13).

LESSON 8: ROMANS 6:1–23

1. *Compare 6:1 with 5:12-21, especially 5:20-21. What is the connection between 5:12-21 and chapter 6?*

Paul's main point in 5:12-21 is: where sin flourished and increased, God's grace abounded all the more. God gave the law so that trespasses might increase—all in order that he might make grace even more overwhelming. Therefore, in chapter 6 the question naturally arises, "Shall we continue in sin now that we are justified so that God's grace will go on increasing?"

2. *What is our relationship, as Christians, to sin? (6:1-2)*

We died to sin.

3. *What does it mean that we were baptized into Christ's death? (6:3-5)*

Baptism represents our identification with Christ in his death and resurrection. (See 4:13-25, note 1; see also 6:1-23, note 2.)

4. *What three things follow from our death with Christ? (6:4-8)*

(a) We have new life in Christ. The "old self" (5:6) is dead. (b) We have the hope of resurrection. Our "bodies of sin" (5:6) will be

purified, glorified, and raised on the last day. (c) We have been freed
from slavery to sin and no longer give in to it (5:7).

5. How could Christ, who never sinned, die to sin? (6:9-10)
He died to sin once for all as the Representative or Substitute for
sinful men.

**6. How can we make our death to sin and our new life to God more
real in our experience? (6:11-13)**
(a) We are to *count ourselves* dead to sin and no longer under its
dominion; and we are to *count ourselves* alive to God. To *count
ourselves* such is simply to believe that God has accomplished it
(even when we do not feel it). (b) We are to *yield our bodies* to God as
those who are spiritually alive. We are to seek his will and to try to
do it, believing that he will enable us to live in faithful obedience to
his law.

**7. Sin must not be our master, because we have died to sin (6:1-13).
Give another reason why sin shall not be our master. (6:14)**
We are no longer under law, which binds us to sin (1 Cor. 15:56),
but under grace, i.e., in the sphere of his special favor. Part of his
grace to us is the power to overcome sin.

**8. What, besides law, can make us sin's slaves? (6:15-16; also Exod.
21:5-6)**
Willing obedience to sin's decrees.

9. What is the outcome of slavery to sin? (6:16)
Death.

**10. How does one become free from sin and a "slave" of righteous-
ness? (6:17-19)**
Obedience to the gospel (6:17; also 1:5).

11. What is the outcome of "slavery" to righteousness? (6:19-23)
Sanctification, holiness, and eternal life.

LESSON 9: Romans 7:1–25

1. Whom is Paul addressing in chapter 7? (7:1)
Paul is addressing his "brothers" who "know the law." He may have in mind primarily his fellow Jewish Christians. However, Christians of Gentile origin must have known the law then just as they do now. So, we ought to take these words as directed to all Christians who know God's Word.

2. What breaks the binding force of a law? (7:1-3)
Death abolishes all legal obligations.

3. Who was once under the law? (7:4)
The Jews were under the law of Moses, but Gentiles also were under law—the law written in their hearts (2:14-15). (See also Gal. 4:5, which suggests that all the redeemed were under law before they were saved.)

4. How did I die to the law? (7:4)
I died to the law when Christ died (2 Cor. 5:14; Gal. 2:20).

5. What was God's purpose in dissolving my obligation to the law—or did he not dissolve it? (7:4-6, 12)
God dissolved my obligation to keep the law under penalty of death. In Christ I have already died the death required of transgressors. I am no longer *under* law (Rom. 6:1-23, note 6). But God dissolved my bond to the law so that, by the power of the Holy Spirit, I might bring forth fruit for him. *The service my new Lord requires consists of the very works that the law prescribes.*

6. Freedom from the law does not mean freedom from serving God. In what new capacity or power do Christians serve him? (7:6)
We serve as those who are alive, free, and empowered by the Spirit of God, not as those who are bound by law to serve.

7. What does the law do in us? (7:5, 7-11)
The law reveals that we are sinners. More than that, it stirs up our sinful natures to commit sin (3:19–5:20).

8. Is the law the source of sin in our lives? (7:12-14)

No. We are already sinful by nature. The sinful nature is the source of the sinful things we do. The law simply gives the sinful nature more opportunities to express itself in transgression and rebellion.

9. Who is speaking in 7:14-24: Saul the unconverted Jew or Paul the Christian?

Paul is writing as a Christian in 7:14-24. Verses 17 and 20 make it clear that Paul does not consider the sin dwelling within him to be the real Paul any longer. (See 7:1-25, note 3, for an extended discussion of this question.)

10. Does 7:25 summarize the best a Christian can hope for in trying to live a holy life in this world?

In chapter 6 Paul made it clear that much more is expected of a believer than 7:25 suggests (see 6:1-2, 11-14, 19-23). Paul is not asserting in 7:25 that the best we can attain is a desire to obey God's law, but that the disobedience and failure we experience is due to the old sinful nature. He will go on in chapter 8 to reassert the blessed truth that what the law requires can and must be worked out in our lives by the power of the Holy Spirit, by whom we can put to death the deeds of our sinful nature.

LESSON 10: Romans 8:1–17

1. What verdict does God pass on those who belong to Christ Jesus? (8:1)

There is no condemnation for them (John 3:18). They are acquitted and justified (3:24; 4:25; 5:1).

2. What do the phrases "the law of the Spirit of life" and "the law of sin and death" mean? (8:2; also 7:6, 14a)

The "law of the Spirit of life" is God's holy will, the same will expressed in his law, now at work in us by the Holy Spirit. We who have been made alive in Christ both desire to do the will of God and are enabled to do it by the power of the Spirit (Jer. 31:31-34; 1 John 2:7-8).

The "law of sin and death" is the will of the unholy sinful nature, which opposes God's holy will. The will of the sinful nature holds the unbeliever in a state of condemnation and death by the rule and dominion it exercises in his or her life. Alternatively (but perhaps less likely), "the law of sin and death" could refer to the law of Moses viewed as an external, written code that men are under and against which they rebel, a law that condemns them to death. (See 2 Cor. 3:5-6; also 8:1-17, note 2.)

3. How did we receive the verdict of "no condemnation"? (8:3)

God condemned our sin in the body of Christ. He received the condemnation we deserved.

4. Why was it impossible to receive such a verdict under the law? (8:3)

The law was weakened by the old sinful nature. The old nature could not and did not want to keep the law of God.

5. What was God's purpose in condemning sin in the body of Christ? (8:3-4)

God's purpose was that the redeemed might glorify him by their obedience to his law, fulfilling its righteous demands by the power of the Holy Spirit.

6. How do the justified live? (8:4-5)

The justified live "according to the Spirit," i.e., under the direction and by the power of the Holy Spirit.

7. How do the justified think? (8:5-6)

They set their minds on the things the Spirit desires.

8. How do the condemned think? (8:6-8)

They set their minds on the things of the sinful nature. Their minds are hostile to God's law.

9. What is the believer's relationship to his sinful nature (or flesh)? (8:9-12)

The believer is not controlled by that nature (literally, "not in the flesh"). The "body," i.e., the old nature, is dead; but the spirit is alive, a new creation (2 Cor. 5:17).

10. How can believers live for God in their mortal bodies, which still bear their old sinful nature? (8:13-14)

(a) By the power of the Holy Spirit we must put to death the deeds belonging to the sinful nature. (b) We must follow the leading of the Holy Spirit. The Spirit moves us and shows us how to obey God's law (see Gal. 5:16-26).

11. What does the Spirit of God do for us in our struggle against sin? (8:13-16)

(a) The Spirit enables us to put to death the deeds of the sinful nature. (b) The Spirit leads us as God's children, showing us what to do and how to live. (c) The Spirit bears witness with our own spirit that we are children of God.

12. What is our relationship to God now that we are Christians? (8:14)

We are God's children. We are no longer slaves, but sons (Gal. 4:7).

13. How can we be assured that we are God's children? (8:15-16)

The Holy Spirit testifies to our spirits that it is so. The Spirit moves us to address God intimately as "Father." The word *Abba* (verse 15) is not Greek, but Aramaic (the language Jesus grew up speaking). It is closer in feeling to the informal "Daddy" than to the formal "Father." The Spirit moves us to speak to God with the same closeness and intimacy that Jesus felt.

14. What hope does this assurance give us? (8:17)

If we are God's sons, we shall be his heirs together with Christ. We know that we shall ultimately share his glory, even though we may suffer for him now (5:2-4).

LESSON 11: ROMANS 8:17–39

1. What do Christians need to experience? Why? (8:17)

We must suffer. The purpose of our suffering is that we may be glorified with Christ (Matt. 5:10-12; 20:21-28; Phil. 1:29; 3:10-11; 2 Tim. 1:8; Heb. 12:2-11; 1 Pet. 1:6-7; 4:13-14).

2. What is Paul's estimate of his present sufferings? (8:18)
They are not worth being compared with the glory that shall be revealed in us.

3. What is the present state of God's creation? (8:19-21)
(a) It eagerly longs for the sons of God to be revealed in glory. (b) It is in bondage to decay and subject to "frustration" (Greek: *mataiotes*, rendered *vanity* in the KJV and *futility* in the RSV). The creation is frustrated, because it neither is nor can be what God intended it to be. It has no meaning in itself and cannot fulfill its original purpose while mankind remains fallen (Eccles. 1:1-11).

4. Why is creation in this state? (8:20)
God made creation subject to decay (Gen. 3:14-19). It was his sovereign will that creation should not achieve fulfillment with sinful man at its head. Yet he cursed creation in hope; see Genesis 3:15b, a prophetic reference to man's victory over Satan through Jesus Christ.

5. How will creation be restored? (8:21)
(a) Creation will be set free from its bondage to decay. (b) It will be brought into the glorious liberty of God's children.

6. What does the future restoration of creation mean for us now? (8:22-25)
It gives us hope. Our bodies will be redeemed, and we will receive the full status, privileges, and powers of the sons of God.

7. What does the Spirit do for us? (8:26-27)
The Spirit helps us pray according to the will of God, interceding for us with groans we cannot put into words.

8. Why is this work of the Spirit necessary? (8:26)
We are weak. We don't know how to pray as we ought to pray.

9. God works in all things for the good of whom? (8:28)
He works in all things for the good of those who love him, for

those whom he has called. In all things he works according to his
purpose.

10. What is God's purpose for those he has chosen? (8:29)
His will is that we should be made to be like his Son.

**11. What chain of events will God use in making people eventually
to be like Christ? (8:29-30)**
Those he foreknew he predestined; those he predestined he
called; those he called he justified, and those he justified he
glorified.

12. What does each of the events or stages in verses 29-30 mean?
(a) *Foreknew:* God chose some, the elect, to be his own (Amos 3:2; 1
Pet. 1:2). (b) *Predestined:* God decreed and established the events
that would come to pass in the life of each of the elect. (c) *Called:* the
Holy Spirit awakens a sense of sin and guilt in the heart of the elect,
reveals Christ to the person, and works faith in his or her heart. (d)
Justified: God declares the penitent, believing sinner guiltless and
righteous on the basis of the work of Christ for him or her. (e)
Glorified: God will fully purge the believer of sin and make the
person holy and righteous like Christ.

13. When does each of the events or stages in verses 29-30 occur?
a. *Foreknew:* before the creation of the world (Eph. 1:4).
b. *Predestined:* also before the creation of the world.
c. *Called:* when the Holy Spirit works in us to create repentance
and faith in Christ.
d. *Justified:* when we put our trust in Christ.
e. *Glorified:* we will be fully glorified at the resurrection.
Note: Paul writes of the calling, justification, and glorification of all
the elect in the past (aorist) tense, i.e., as an accomplished fact, even
though part of the elect have not yet been born, some of the elect
now living have not yet been called and justified, and none of the
elect have yet been resurrected. He uses the past tense because of
the certainty that God will bring to pass all that he has decreed.
What God purposes to do is as good as done.

14. What are the implications of verses 28-30 for the present? (8:31-34)·
We can have confidence that he who began a good work in us will

surely bring it to completion on the day of Jesus Christ (Phil. 1:6). We can be confident that God works in all things for our good in spite of appearances to the contrary. He planned our lives from before the creation of the world. He will not abandon his purpose for us or forsake us.

15. Jesus said that many would lose their faith and fall away in times of persecution (Matt. 24:9-13). Can you reconcile that statement with 8:35-39?

Read in context and in the light of other passages of God's Word, it seems clear that Jesus' words in Matthew 24:9-13 describe those who outwardly appear to believe but do not actually have genuine faith (Matt. 24: 22-24; see also Phil. 1:6; 2 Pet. 2:9; 1 John 2:18-19). The elect, those whom the Father has given to the Son, are effectually called and truly believe, and these will never fall away (John 6:37-40). Jesus prayed that the faith of the elect would never fail (John 17:6-12). We can be sure that the Father has answered and will continue to answer that prayer.

LESSON 12: ROMANS 9:1–29

1. What is Paul's attitude toward the Jews? (9:1-3)

He is sincerely anguished over their unbelief, for they are his kinsmen. He feels such solidarity with them that he could even wish to be cut off from Christ if it could result in their salvation (compare with Exod. 32:32).

2. What blessings had God given the Jews? (9:4-5)

a. *Sonship* (Exod. 4:22; Deut. 14:1; 32:4-5; Isa. 64:8; Jer. 3:9; Hos. 1:10; 11:1; John 8:41).

b. *Glory* (Exod. 16:10; 24:16; 40:34-38; Lev. 9:6; 1 Kings 8:11; Zech. 2:4-5).

c. *Covenants* (Gen. 15:18; 17:2; Exod. 2:24; 6:2-4; 34:10; Deut. 4:31; 5:2; 7:9; 1 Chron. 16:14-18).

d. *The law* (Exod. 24:12; Deut. 4:8; Pss. 1:1-2; 119; 147:19-20; Acts 7:53).

e. *Worship ordinances* (Deut. 12; Heb. 9:1-6).

f. *Promises* (Gen. 22:15-18; 26:1-5; 28:13-15; 2 Chron. 20:7; Isa.

41:8; Mal. 1:2; John 8:39,52-53; Heb. 11:8-12).

g. *The Messiah*, or *Christ* (Gen. 49:10; 2 Sam. 7:12-14a; 1 Chron. 17:11-14; Pss. 2; 72; Isa. 52:13-53; Mic. 5:2; John 4:22).

3. Why might someone think that "God's word had failed"? (9:6)

The great majority of Jews in Paul's day had rejected Jesus as their Messiah. For the most part they have continued in unbelief down to the present day. Those who reject their Messiah have forfeited the blessings promised to the patriarchs *and their descendants*. Can man reject God's promised salvation and thereby make God a liar? And what about the assurance, founded on God's foreknowledge and love, of which Paul writes so eloquently in chapter 8? If God had permitted his people of old to fall away through unbelief, how can *we* be secure? Can man's unbelief make God's promise of no effect? (3:3)

4. How does Paul answer the charge that God was not true to his word? (9:6-13)

Not all who are Jews by physical descent are true Jews, i.e., descendants of Abraham whom God counts as heirs of the promise. God's purpose included the choice, or *election* of some to be his people. The rest were not chosen.

5. What are God's criteria for choosing and blessing someone? (9:14-16)

God asserts his right to be merciful to whom he chooses, giving no other reasons than his own will (Exod. 33:19).

6. What does this passage say about a man's will? (9:16-18)

Salvation does not depend at all on a man's will or choice. It is due solely to the sovereign mercy of God (see also John 1:13).

7. What objections are raised to Paul's conclusions? (9:19)

(a) It would be unjust of God to elect some and not others (9:14). (b) How can God condemn people for failing to repent and believe if he is in complete control of their destiny? (9:19)

8. How does Paul answer those objections? (9:20-21)

God has the right to condemn a sinner for his sins; he also has the right to save a sinner from his sins. God is our Creator and has the right—not simply the power, but also the right—to do with any of his creatures as he pleases. At this point in his argument Paul does not seek to reconcile God's absolute right to elect whom he pleases with his infinite love, but by the time he concludes this portion of Romans he will have entirely vindicated the love of God as worked out in his purpose of election.

9. What ends has God destined or prepared people to serve? (9:22-23)
Some are destined to show the glory of God as he executes his wrath on them because of their sin. Others are destined to show the glory of God as he has mercy on them by saving them from sin and glorifying them with Christ.

10. Do both ends show forth the power and glory of God? If so, how?
Yes. God shows his holiness in punishing sin and bringing the evildoer to judgment (Pss. 2; 9:1-7; 15–17; Jer. 23:5; Joel 3:11-12; Rev. 14:7; 16:7), and he shows his love and goodness in justifying and glorifying the elect (1 Chron. 16:34-35; Eph. 1:3-14).

11. Why hasn't God already executed judgment on the "objects of his wrath"? (9:22-23)
God is very patient, waiting for all the elect "objects of his mercy" to be saved. (See also Matt. 13:24-30, especially verses 28-29, and 2 Pet. 3:9.)

12. Whom did God choose to be the "objects of his mercy"? (9:23-26)
He chose both Jews and Gentiles.

13. Considering the fact that only a few Jews turned to Christ, are we to think of God as hard in electing only a few or as merciful in electing some? Or is there some other way to view the fact that God has elected but a remnant of Israel? (9:27-29)
Paul's emphasis is on sovereign *grace*. If God were not merciful, not even a remnant would be saved (9:29). But why not a larger remnant? Why doesn't God extend his mercy to all Jews, indeed, to all the world? Answers to these questions are not found in Romans 9. But chapter 9 must not be read in isolation. Paul goes on in chapters 10 and 11 to show how the small remnant of saved Jews in

his day (and ours) is part of God's plan for the salvation of "all Israel" (11:26) as well as an innumerable multitude from all nations.

LESSON 13: ROMANS 9:30–10:21

1. The Jews sought righteousness, but most of them failed to obtain it. Why? (9:30–10:3)

The Jews pursued a righteousness based on works of the law rather than a righteousness based on faith in Christ. They sought to establish their *own* righteousness rather than submitting to the righteousness that *God* provides.

2. Has Paul written off Israel? Has he consigned them to the wrath of God? (10:1)

No. He prays to God for their salvation.

3. What human action is involved in discovering and appropriating God's way of being justified? (10:4-10)

One must *believe* the facts of the gospel—especially the truth that God raised Jesus from the dead, for that act validated the entire gospel message (see 1:4; also Acts 17:31; 1 Cor. 15:1-20). One must *confess* Jesus Christ as Lord, i.e., as *Kurios*, Jehovah, God Almighty (see 1:1-17, note 4). Paul comments on Deuteronomy 30:12-14 to reinforce his point that the righteousness of faith does not doubt that Christ is God come down from heaven ("Who will ascend into heaven?") or that he rose from the dead ("Who will descend into the deep?"), but instead confesses that the risen Christ is Lord. (See Matt. 10:33; 1 John 2:22-23; 4:2, 15.)

4. How can an individual make sure that he or she is one of the elect, one of those whom God has called to be an "object of mercy"? (10:9-12)

One has only to *call on him*. God will save everyone, Jew or Gentile, who calls on the name of the Lord Jesus Christ (Acts 4:10-12; 2 Pet. 1:10).

5. What prevents men from calling on the Lord? (10:14-17)

They do not call on him, because they do not believe in him. They do not believe in him, because they have never heard the gospel. They have not heard the gospel, because there is no one sent by God to announce the gospel to them (but see answer to question 7).

6. What can we do to awaken faith in Christ within the unconverted? (10:17)

We can preach and teach the Word of Christ. The gospel message creates its own faith: faith comes by hearing, and hearing by the preaching of Christ.

7. Can anyone plead ignorance as an excuse for not responding to the gospel? Explain. (10:18)

No. "All the earth" has heard. Paul is referring to Jews scattered throughout the known world. The essentials of the gospel were proclaimed in the Old Testament. Israel had no excuse for not recognizing and believing in Jesus as the Christ. (See 9:30–10:21, note 4.)

8. What was Israel's attitude toward the gospel and toward the fact that the Gentiles had accepted it? (10:19-21)

Israel was envious and angry (verse 19), disobedient and obstinate (verse 21).

LESSON 14: ROMANS 11:1–36

1. Has God rejected Israel? Justify your answer. (11:1-6)

No, God has not rejected his ancient people (1 Sam. 12:22; Jer. 31:37). Paul cites four reasons for his confidence: (a) He is an Israelite himself, of the tribe of Benjamin. (b) God *foreknew* Israel. Those whom God foreknew and chose before the creation of the world (Eph. 1:4) are sure to be saved (Rom. 8:28-30). (c) The history of Israel shows that God preserves a remnant for himself, even when it appears to human eyes that his people have irrevocably rejected him. (d) There is a remnant of believing Jews even today, saved by grace through faith in Christ.

2. In the final analysis, what has kept the mass of Jews from receiving the gospel? (11:7-10)

God has hardened them. He has made their minds dull, their eyes blind to spiritual truth, and their ears deaf to the gospel. This hardening is judicial, i.e., punishment for their sins (1:28), but it is also intended to further God's redemptive purpose in the world.

3. What is God's purpose in hardening most of Israel? (11:11-12)
God's intention is to use Israel's unbelief to bring salvation to the Gentiles.

4. What has resulted from the unbelief of the Jews? (11:12, 30-32)
The Gentile world has heard the gospel, and many Gentiles have believed and received mercy. This is exactly the result God intended.

5. What has resulted from the salvation of the Gentiles? (11:14, 19)
The Jews have been made jealous (see Acts 17:5).

6. What will result at last from the jealousy of Israel? {11:15-16, 26, 31)
The Jews as a people will again receive mercy and be saved.

7. Paul warns against an attitude that Gentile Christians might harbor toward the Jews. (11:17-24)

a. What is that attitude?
Pride and conceit.

b. Why is it wrong?
In addition to the fact that pride and conceit are sins (1:30), such pride is wrong because Gentile Christians have not been saved *instead of* Israel, but rather *as part of* Israel. The church is not God's *new* people; rather, it is God's *ancient* people into which individual Gentiles have been incorporated by faith.

c. Why is it dangerous?
We stand only through faith. We must continue in faith to receive the promise (Heb. 3:4). Pride is a threat to faith. It puts us in danger of falling into sin and can lead to spiritual destruction (Prov. 16:18; 1 Cor. 10:6, 11-12; James 4:6-7).

8. What secret does Paul reveal to his readers? (11:25-32)

Only part of Israel has been hardened, and that only for a limited time. God intends the hardening of Israel to result in the salvation of the elect Gentiles. When the full number of elect Gentiles have been saved, God will save all Israel (Rev. 7:1-12).

9. Why does he reveal this secret? (11:25, 33-36)

(a) He wants to squelch any conceit on the part of his Gentile readers. (b) He wants his readers to perceive in some measure the depth of God's wisdom and knowledge, so that they might join him in adoration and praise of God for his plan of salvation.

LESSON 15: ROMANS 12:1–21

1. What is a sacrifice? (Exod. 20:24; Lev. 1:7-9; Deut. 12:27)

A *sacrifice* is a gift or life offered to God. It must be without defect or blemish (Mal. 1:8).

2. What does it mean for us to offer our bodies as "living sacrifices"? (12:1; also 6:12-13; 8:1-14)

We are to live for God, not for ourselves or for anyone or anything else. We are to consider our old selves dead and our new selves holy and acceptable to God through the cleansing blood of Christ (1 Pet. 1:2; Rev. 1:5). We live for God by seeking to know what is "good, pleasing and perfect" according to his will and by doing it.

3. How can we know what is God's "good, pleasing and perfect will" for us? (12:2)

Our minds must be transformed from conformity to this world and its way of looking at things to conformity to God's will and God's viewpoint (Eph. 4:22-24; 5:10, 17).

4. What are the characteristics of a renewed, transformed mind? (12:3)

(a) It is not conceited: we ought not to think more highly of ourselves than is warranted. (b) It is objective about one's self: we ought to view ourselves with "sober judgment" (verse 3). (c) It has faith in one's ability to serve the Lord and his church: we ought to view ourselves as gifted by God in some special way for the benefit of the church.

5. What relationship do Christians have to one another? To what does Paul compare our relationship? (12:4-5)

We are *members* of one another in the original sense of that word; we are like limbs and organs of the same body. We all belong to the church of Christ, which Paul elsewhere describes as his body (Eph. 5:23). We have different gifts and abilities from God to use for the good of all the members individually and collectively. We are to live in submission to the head of the body, Jesus Christ (see also 1 Cor. 12:12-27).

6. Why does God give us gifts? (12:6-8)

God is *gracious* to us. He delights to show his favor to us and to do us good (1 Cor. 12:7).

7. What are we to do with the gifts God has given us? (12:6-8)

We are to *use* them, not for personal ends but for the benefit of the church and the glory of God.

8. How can you find out what your own gifts are? (12:3)

Think realistically and objectively about your abilities. Be neither conceited, thinking more highly about yourself than you ought, nor lacking the faith to recognize that God has given you gifts. Seek the insight of mature Christians whose wisdom, knowledge, and leadership you know to be of God (verse 8; also 1 Cor. 12:5). They may be able to help you identify your gifts. (See 12:1-21, note 3.)

9. What motivates us to use the gifts we have received? (12:1-5)

(a) The desire to live for God and not for self, i.e., willingness to be a "living sacrifice," (b) The faith that we do have gifts and that we can live a holy, God-pleasing life; the conviction that we can know God's will and do it.

10. What hinders us from using these gifts? (12:3b, 6b)

(a) Self-centeredness: preoccupation with our own interests. (b) Weak faith: inability or unwillingness to believe that we have received gifts from God for the benefit of the church, that we can know God's will, and that we can do his will in his power.

11. What attitudes are we to cultivate toward fellow Christians? (12:9-13, 16; also Gal. 5:19-26, especially verses 22-26)
(a) Love that is genuine and sincere. (b) Hatred of evil: the desire to see the church pure and holy. (c) Prizing the good: seeking the church's good and that of the cause of Christ. (d) Loving devotion to our brothers and sisters in the Lord. (e) Striving to honor other believers. (f) A zeal for Christ and his kingdom that cannot be extinguished. (g) Being aglow with the Spirit (or fervent in spirit) as we serve Christ. (h) Joy and hope in Christ. (i) Faithfulness in prayer for God's people. (j) Patience in affliction suffered for Christ. (k) Sharing what we have with brothers and sisters in need. (l) Seeking occasions to show hospitality to brothers and sisters in the Lord. (m) Sympathy, or fellow-feeling: rejoicing with those who rejoice and mourning with those who mourn. (n) Harmony: striving to get along in peaceful cooperation with fellow Christians. (o) Humility: willingness to associate with those of low status or position.

As we read 12:9-13, we ought to bear in mind that: (a) The Greek words in these verses denoting the various attitudes and practices we should cultivate are translated quite differently in the various English versions in common use today. (b) The attitudes and practices commended here all have reference to our relations with other Christians, to life in the family of God. For example, although we are to hate all evil, the admonition to hate what is evil in verse 9 refers primarily to evil in the church.

12. What attitudes are we to cultivate toward our neighbors, whether they are fellow Christians or not? (12:14-21)
In addition to the attitudes and practices listed in answer 11, we are to seek to live at peace with unbelievers. As much as lies in our power we must avoid strife. We are neither to avenge ourselves when wronged nor to wish ill to those who mistreat or hate us. We are rather to do good to those who do us ill and pray for them (Matthew 5:38-48). We are to do what is good in the sight of all men, i.e., to observe commonly acknowledged standards of courtesy, decency, charity, and social behavior as long as these standards do

not conflict with the law of God.

13. Can we expect to get along well with our neighbors and our fellow Christians when we live according to Paul's admonitions? (12:14-21)

We will avoid most strife with unbelievers when we live a life pleasing to the Lord. Still, we cannot avoid all strife. Some trouble is inevitable precisely because we seek to live godly lives for Christ Jesus (Matt. 5:11-12,43-44; John 15:18-21; 2 Tim. 1:8; 3:12; 1 Pet. 3:10-14).

LESSON 16: Romans 13:1–14

1. How are we to regard or view the governing authorities? (13:1-2, 4)

The sovereign Lord instituted governments among men. Whatever governments exist are established by him (but see 13:1-14, note 3). God established governments for our good. He has authorized and charged them to execute his wrath upon evildoers and to do us good. God will hold governments accountable and will judge them according to their faithfulness in carrying out the duties he has laid upon them. (See 1 Kings 3:7-9; 8:25; 11:9-11; Prov. 16:10-15, especially verse 12b; and 20:26,28.)

2. How are we to behave toward the governing authorities? (13:1-7)

We are to submit to them. We must not only obey because of the force they can employ to exact obedience; we must also regard their authority over us as legitimate. Hence, we are not to resist or rebel against their authority. We are to do right by obeying the laws and by paying taxes; we are also to give them honor and respect. Although Paul does not mention it here, in 1 Timothy 2:1-2 he tells us to pray for our leaders so that they will carry out the duties with which God has charged them; for in so doing they make it possible for us to live peaceful and quiet lives in obedience to God. (See also 1 Sam. 24:1-6; 26:7-11; 1 Tim. 2:1-2; Titus 3:1; 1 Pet. 2:13-17.)

3. What is the proper, God-ordained role of government? (13:3-6)

(a) Government is obligated to punish those who do evil, using force when necessary. When the governing authorities do this, they accomplish two things: (1) They act as God's agents in executing his judgment on the wicked. (2) They make the world a safe place where we can go about the business of living for God.

(b) Government is God's agent for our good (verse 4). Does this role give the state a mandate to undertake activities that "promote the general welfare" (as written in the preamble to the Constitution of the United States of America) when those activities are not directly related to defense and public safety? What of activities such as education, the care of orphans, and public works? Paul does not address such questions here. (See 13:1-14, note 2 for further discussion.)

4. What kind of debts are we permitted to incur (13:8ff.)

We are to have no outstanding debts except the continuing debt to love one another—a debt that can never be paid in full.

5. What is the role of the law for the Christian? (13:8-10)

We are obligated to keep the law of God in that we are obligated to love our neighbor. The law shows us what loving behavior is. All the commandments Paul cites here illustrate the love that will not do anything to harm its neighbor. (See also Lev. 19:18; Matt. 22:34-40; Luke 10:29-37; John 14:15, 21; 15:9-13; Gal. 5:14; 6:2.)

6. What reason does Paul give here for encouraging his readers to live God's way rather than the world's way? (13:11-14)

The return of Christ is getting closer every day. His return means our salvation (in the sense of salvation from the world) and glorification (see also 1 John 3:2-3).

7. How can we live God's way? (13:14)

We are to *clothe* ourselves with the Lord Jesus Christ and not to think about how to gratify the desires of the sinful nature (Greek: *sarx*; see 6:1-23, note 4). To *clothe* ourselves with Christ is simply to yield ourselves to him, choosing to live holy and pleasing lives in the power of the Holy Spirit, so that we *live as he did*. See Colossians 3:1-14, where the metaphor of *putting off* the sinful nature and *putting on* holy behavior is expanded. (The Greek word for *clothe* in Rom. 13:14 and the words for *put on* and *clothe* in Col. 3:10 and 12 are all forms of the same verb.) Paul has already exhorted us to this forsaking of sin and living for God in similar terms in Romans 6:11-13; 8:9-13; and 12:1-2.

LESSON 17: ROMANS 14:1–23

1. What does weak in faith mean? (14:1-2, 14, 23)

The *faith* referred to here is not trust in Christ or belief in the cardinal doctrines of the Bible. It is belief that Christ has freed us from the ceremonial law and from human regulations (see also 1 Cor. 8:7; Gal. 5:13-15; Col. 2:16-17, 20-22). To be *weak in faith* is to have a weak conscience, i.e., one that condemns for doing something not actually forbidden by God's law or for failing to do something not actually commanded by the moral law.

2. What matters were disputed in the church at Rome? (14:2, 5, 14-17)

(a) Are some foods morally unclean? May one eat meat as well as vegetables (14:2, 14)? (b) Should certain days be observed as holy days or are all days alike (verse 5; also Gal. 4:10)? (c) Is it permissible to drink wine (14:21)?

3. In general, how are we to behave toward those weak in faith? (14:1, 3, 10, 13-15, 19-21)

(a) We should accept them without passing judgment or arguing about debatable matters (14:1, 10). (b) We ought not to despise them (14:3, 10). (c) We should resolve not to put an obstacle or stumbling block in their way, i.e., we should not let our actions destroy the weaker brother or lead him into sin (14:13-15).

4. What is Paul's admonition to the restrictive Christian?

(a) He is not to judge and condemn his more permissive brothers (14:3). (b) He must not do anything his conscience does not permit (14:23).

5. What is Paul's command to all Christians, restrictive and permissive? (14:1, 4-12, 13, 18, 19)

(a) We are to welcome one another in spite of the kinds of differences described in this passage (14:1, 3). (b) We are not to pass judgment on one another (14:4,10,13). (c) We are to live for the Lord: whatever we do or refrain from doing is to be for God (14:6-9). We are to remember that we will have to give account to him of how we lived (14:12). (d) We are to pursue righteousness and peace and joy in the power of the Holy Spirit (14:18). (e) We are to do whatever we can to promote peace and mutual upbuilding (14:19).

6. *Why is it wrong to judge a brother's convictions about the kinds of issues under consideration here? (14:8-13a)*

Our unspiritual tendency is to judge our brother rather than his convictions. Our brother is accountable to God, not to us. Every Christian is to live unto the Lord and not unto men, not even fellow Christians. God will judge our brother—and us as well.

7. *What constraints limit a Christian's liberty of conduct? (see also 13:8-14).*

We are to act out of love for our brothers. We ought to have more concern for their good than for our own pleasure or liberty.

8. *What is wrong with continuing in certain behavior that I know is acceptable to God, even good in itself, when a less mature, weaker brother considers it to be sinful? (14:19-21)*

(a) Continuing in such practices can lead to divisions in the church and destroy peace among believers. (b) Our conduct can destroy the weaker brother by encouraging him to engage in behavior that his conscience does not really approve. To practice what the conscience does not allow is sin (14:23), and persistence in sin against one's conscience leads to the shipwreck of one's faith (1 Tim. 1:19).

9. *Can you think of contemporary issues in the church to which this chapter is especially applicable?*

The use of alcohol and vegetarianism, mentioned here, are still disputed issues in various quarters of the church. Some would say that honoring the Lord's Day is also a disputable matter; however, while it may be disputed, it ought not to be (see 14:1-23, note 4). Examples of other disputed matters are the issue of paying taxes that support state-financed abortions or military expenditures considered unjust by the taxpayer, membership in certain fraternal organizations or labor unions, the use of tobacco, social dancing, and partici-

pation in Halloween activities. Many other disputed practices could
be cited.

LESSON 18: ROMANS 15:1–33

**1. What principles should govern our behavior toward our fellow
believers? (15:1-2, 5, 7-8)**

(a) We ought to bear with their failings and weaknesses and not
live only to please ourselves. (b) We should please our neighbor in
what we do if that will promote his good and edification. (c) We
must try to live in harmony with each other. (d) We must accept each
other as we are now. (e) We ought to follow the Lord's example and
view ourselves as servants of our fellow Christians.

**2. How did Jesus illustrate and exemplify these principles? (15:3-8;
see also Matt. 12:20)**

(a) Christ did not live for himself, but for God. (b) He accepted the
insults that were directed toward God. Such insults are bound to be
flung at those who live for God (John 15:18-21). (c) He welcomed us
and accepted us into God's people even though we were (and are)
sinners. (d) He became a servant to God's people.

**3. Paul quotes Psalm 69:7-9 in verse 3. What is the significance of
this verse for Paul's argument?**

Paul states that this Scripture was given so that we might receive
encouragement and be made patient, so that we might live in hope.
We can expect that living as servants of our neighbor and of God will
lead to insult and reproach. But God glorified Christ after his obedience and suffering, and he will glorify us also (2 Cor. 1:3-7; 1 Pet.
5:10).

4. What enables us to glorify God together? (15:5-6)

Unity in following Christ.

5. Why should we accept each other? (15:7)

Christ has accepted every one of us.

6. What is Paul's purpose in quoting the Old Testament in verses

8-13? What is the function of those quotations in his argument?
(a) Paul wants to reinforce the truth just stated (15:7) that Christ welcomed the "weaker," i.e., the Gentile, into God's people. We should serve God as Christ did, by accepting the weaker brother into our fellowship without looking down on him or wrangling with him (14:1-3). (b) He wants to encourage the Gentile Christians in Rome and to build up their confidence and hope. (c) He wants Gentile believers to praise God for his mercy to them in Christ. (d) He wishes to introduce the concluding section of the letter. Paul's conclusion deals with his ministry to the Gentiles.

7. Paul has a high view of the knowledge and maturity of the Christians in Rome. Why then does he write such a long doctrinal letter to them? (15:14-15; also 1:11-12; 16:17-19).
(a) Paul wants to remind them of some particular points (15:14-15). (b) He has an obligation to the Romans as well as to the rest of the Gentiles. Paul is obligated to make sure that the Roman church receives the full counsel of God even though they have heard the gospel from other sources (1:11-12).

8. What were Paul's goals as a minister of Christ? (15:16,19,20)
Paul sought to proclaim the gospel to the Gentiles, particularly where it had not been preached before. He also endeavored to make his converts "an offering acceptable to God, sanctified by the Holy Spirit" (verse 16)—in other words, mature Christians.

9. What were Paul's means in proclaiming the gospel? (15:18-19; see also 1 Cor. 1:17; 2:1-5)
Paul preached the gospel. In the course of his preaching he also performed signs and miracles that confirmed the message (Acts 13:9-12; 14:8-10; 17:25-29; 19:6; 20:9-12; 28:1-6). The preaching, the signs, and the miracles were all done in the power of the Holy Spirit.

10. How much of the task that God had given him had Paul completed at the time he wrote Romans? (15:22-24)
Paul had "fully proclaimed" the gospel of Christ all the way from Jerusalem to Illyricum (the coastal region of modern Yugoslavia). There was no more work for an *apostle* in those regions (see 15:1-33, note 3).

11. What work remained for Paul to accomplish? (15:24-28)

Paul wanted to preach the gospel in Spain, the farthest reach of the empire in his day. He first had to carry a donation from the churches of Macedonia and Achaia (Greece) to the poor among the saints in Jerusalem. He intended afterward to visit Rome en route to Spain.

12. How could the Christians at Rome be Paul's co-workers? (15:24-33)

(a) Paul hoped they would be able to assist him on his journey to Spain. Whether he had financial help in mind in addition to hospitality is not clear from Romans 15. (b) He wanted them to join him in prayer for his journey to Jerusalem.

LESSON 19: ROMANS 16:1–27

1. Who was Phoebe, and what was her relationship to Paul and to the church at Rome? (16:1-2)

Phoebe was a servant or, possibly, a deaconess (see 16:1-27, note 1) of the church at Cenchrea, the port of Corinth. Paul wrote Romans from Corinth, and Phoebe apparently carried Paul's letter from there to Rome.

2. Who were Priscilla and Aquila? (16:3-5; see also Acts 18:1-4)

Priscilla and Aquila were a Jewish couple who practiced the same trade, tentmaking or leather working, as Paul. They had lived in Corinth for a time after the Emperor Claudius had expelled the Jews from Rome, and Paul lived and worked with them while they were there. A church had met in their house in Corinth, and a church was meeting in their house in Rome at the time Paul wrote his letter.

3. Was Paul personally acquainted with all those he greets in verses 3-15?

He definitely knew Epenetus, Andronicus and Junia, Ampliatus, Urbanus, Stachys, Herodian, Persis, and Rufus. It is possible he knew all those he addresses by name.

4. What is Paul's warning to the church at Rome? (16:17-20)

The believers there are to be on the watch for men who would cause divisions and teach false doctrine.

5. **Why do some persons create divisions in the church and teach false doctrine? (16:18; see also 1 Tim. 6:3-5; Titus 1:10-11)**
Some do these things because they hope for worldly rewards such as money, adulation and praise, and power.

6. **How can the church ward off division and error? (16:17b, 19-20, 25)**
(a) The church must watch out for those who would divide the fellowship or teach a different gospel. (b) The church must be grounded in the essentials of the gospel.

7. **Paul writes in verses 25-26 of "the revelation of the mystery hidden for long ages past, but now revealed and made known through the prophetic writings by the command of the eternal God, so that all nations might believe and obey him."**

a. **What is "the mystery hidden for long ages past"? (see also Eph. 1:9-10; Col. 1:25-27)**
The mystery is that God intends to save men and women out of all nations through faith in Christ. Although a few Gentiles shared the faith of Israel (Melchizedek, Ruth, and Naaman come to mind), salvation in Christ was virtually unknown to the Gentiles "for long ages past." The fact that God would accept the Gentiles on a completely equal footing with the Jews, the fact that all men are saved through faith in him without works of the law—these truths were largely if not entirely hidden from Jew and Gentile alike.

b. **How has the mystery been "revealed and made known through the prophetic writings by command of the eternal God"?**
The Lord Jesus sent his apostles into all the world to proclaim that the salvation promised by the prophets to Israel was for all nations, that all men could be saved through faith in him.

APPENDIX C
Selected Reference Works

Cranfield, C.E.B. *Romans: A Shorter Commentary*. Grand Rapids: Wm. B. Eerdmans Publishing Co., 1985. This work is an abridgment of Cranfield's two-volume commentary, which appeared in 1975. The discussion of the Greek text has been removed for the most part; the remainder is a clear, comprehensive commentary on the English text of Romans.

Denney, James, "St. Paul's Epistle to the Romans," in W. Robertson Nicoll, ed. *The Expositor's Greek Testament*, vol. 2. Grand Rapids: Wm. B. Eerdmans Publishing Co., reprinted 1983. One need not know Greek to profit from Denney's English introduction to Romans. He deals with the origin of the church at Rome, the character of the Roman church, the occasion and purpose of the letter, and the integrity of the text in concise, evangelical fashion.

Murray, John, *The Epistle to the Romans*. Grand Rapids: Wm. B. Eerdmans Publishing Co., 1968. One volume edition. Murray's commentary is not light reading, but it is worth the effort required to work through it. Murray deals exhaustively with every side of every disputed point and nearly always comes up with conclusive arguments for and against the various interpretations advanced. Murray writes from a decidedly Calvinistic perspective.

APPENDIX D
Index of Study Notes

Spiritual Gifts. 12:1-21, note 3, p. 122.

Submission to the Governing Authorities: Always? 13:1-14, note 3, p. 131.

Suffering in the Life of the Christian. 5:1-21, note 2, p. 48.

The Testimony of Scripture. 2:17–3:20, note 3, p. 25.

"Under law" (6:14). 6:1-23, note 6, p. 61.

The Unsearchable Ways of God. 11:1-36, note 6, p. 113.

"We also rejoice in God" (5:11). 5:1-21, note 3, p. 48.

What Is at Stake: The Faithfulness of God. 11:1-36, note 1, p. 107.

Why Only a Remnant? 11:1-36, note 3, p. 109.

Why Vegetarianism? 14:1-23, note 3, p. 141.

The Wrath of God. 1:18–2:16, note 2, p. 15.

The "wretched man" of Romans 7: Saul or Paul? 7:1-25, note 4, p. 65.

"You will heap burning coals on his head" (12:20). 12:1-21, note 5, p. 125.